DELICIOUS
GATHERINGS

TARATEASPOON

DELICIOUS
GATHERINGS

RECIPES TO CELEBRATE TOGETHER

TARA BENCH

SHADOW
MOUNTAIN
PUBLISHING

Photography by Ty Mecham
Prop Styling by Veronica Olson (except as noted below)
Pages viii, 97, 157, 207, 227, 243: Food Styling by Lindsay Hargett and Shannon Johnson & Prop Styling by
    Carrie Oliver and Charity Olsen

Visit us at shadowmountain.com

Library of Congress Cataloging-in-Publication Data

Names: Bench, Tara, author.
Title: Delicious gatherings : recipes to celebrate together / Tara Bench.
Description: Salt Lake City : Shadow Mountain, [2022] | Includes index. | Summary: "Popular blogger
    Tara Teaspoon shares her favorite recipes that are perfect for large gatherings, family parties, and holiday
    festivities"—Provided by publisher.
Identifiers: LCCN 2022009272 | ISBN 9781639930456 (hardback)
Subjects: LCSH: Cooking, American. | BISAC: COOKING / Entertaining | COOKING / Courses &
    Dishes / General | LCGFT: Cookbooks.
Classification: LCC TX715 .B46574 2022 | DDC 641.5973—dc23/eng/20220404
LC record available at https://lccn.loc.gov/2022009272

Printed in the United States of America
Jostens, Clarksville, TN

10 9 8 7 6 5 4 3 2 1

FOR MY FAMILY. I LOVE BEING
IN THE KITCHEN WITH YOU.

AND FOR MY OTHER "FAMILY"
OF TARA TEASPOON READERS.
I'M HONORED TO BE IN YOUR HOME.

CONTENTS

INTRODUCTION

DELICIOUS GATHERINGS: A PASSION

I have always loved being in the middle of the kitchen action. I was drawn to the hustle and bustle of the kitchen from a young age, and I adored helping my mom, my dad, and my grandmothers cook. My memories are made up of the smells, tastes, and meal moments of childhood.

I am so passionate about the power of food and cooking, and how it can bring people together, allow us to explore our creativity, and nourish our bodies and souls. Cooking is a life skill that can also be enjoyable, not a chore. I want to make cooking fun for everyone, just like it is for me.

This cookbook is meant to inspire you and your family and friends to eat together. The recipes were created to make sharing them easy, so they are easily doubled or cut in half, depending on the size of your gathering. And since connecting over a wonderful meal shouldn't be stressful, in the very first chapter, I've taken the work off your plate, if you will, and created entire menus for you to follow. There's no need to piece ideas together to create a cohesive, delicious meal—unless you want to, of course.

Use the other recipes in the book to plan family weeknight meals, fun weekend cook-alongs with friends, or Sunday and holiday meals to remember. Each recipe is great as part of a bigger meal or can be made individually when you just want a simple soup or a comforting bowl of pasta.

Whatever you cook, I hope you'll enjoy your time in the kitchen and be proud of creating something tasty to share and savor.

I've included a few of the tips and notes I'd share with you if I were visiting you in your kitchen. With this book in your hands, I kind of feel like I am! Thank you for bringing these recipes into your home.

SUCCESS SECRETS

One of the best ways to ensure success is if you read a recipe through before starting to cook. I like to read the recipe even before I make my grocery list! Taking a few minutes to familiarize yourself with a new-to-you recipe allows you to visualize the actions in each step. It builds confidence even before you start and helps your mind note when you'll be adding ingredients, heating the grill, reserving extra pasta water, and things like that.

MISE EN PLACE

Mise en place, roughly translated from French, means "to have everything in place." I use the term in cooking to note that the ingredients should be out and at hand, the equipment needed is gathered and clean, and the space ready before you start making a recipe. I guarantee you will enjoy cooking more if you put a little time into this preparation.

WEIGHTS AND MEASURES

In the United States, we don't rely on our kitchen scale very much to weigh ingredients. But I'm going to suggest you keep one handy in order to weigh your ingredients to be precise—for example, weighing flour in grams instead of cups. There are many affordable models if you'd like to invest in a scale.

In the book, I've included weights for ingredients when it might be helpful for shopping or to help you be successful in cooking. When you are at the store, how do you know if that block of cheese will be 2 cups of shredded cheese? By giving you pounds or ounces, you will know how much to buy before prepping and cooking.

Weighing ingredients, like flour, while cooking or baking, ensures accuracy. Whether you scoop, spoon, sift, or fluff your flour before you add it to the recipe, it will always be a different weight. Meaning, you may unknowingly be adding a few teaspoons extra flour—or up to ¼ cup—to a recipe!

You can still use a measuring cup for flour, but I've included weights where it will help if you'd rather use a scale instead.

SALTED OR UNSALTED

Butter, how I love thee! And salted butter is divine when spread on a slice of bread. That being said, I always keep unsalted butter around because that's what we cooked with in the professional test kitchens I've worked in.

There are a few reasons unsalted butter is used for testing recipes. Salt is not only tasty, but it is also a preservative, meaning salted butter can actually stay on store shelves longer. Buying unsalted butter ensures the butter is fresher. You can also purchase unsalted butter in bulk and keep it in the freezer to preserve the freshness at home.

Unsalted butter is also used in recipe testing because it allows the cook more control over how much salt is going into the recipe. I also use unsalted butter in baking because I like to salt my baked goods with care—just enough salt to bring out the flavors but not so much that my buttery frostings are almost savory!

For more recipes, tips on halving or doubling recipes, and delicious reasons to gather, visit me at TaraTeaspoon.com

In this book, I have specified unsalted butter only where I think it's necessary to have more control over the seasonings, or if I'm baking. If it's not specified, feel free to use whatever butter you have on hand. You can always "season to taste" with salt.

TOOLS AND TIPS

I love a good small appliance, kitchen tool, or helpful kitchen gadget. Over the years, I have only kept the ones I use and think are important so my kitchen doesn't become too cluttered.

In my first cookbook, *Live Life Deliciously*, I shared detailed recommendations for pots and pans, knives, various tools, blenders, food processors, and more. That information is applicable to this cookbook as well.

I've provided tips throughout this book for the use of kitchen tools, like shortcuts using an Instant Pot, using a mandoline to slice or julienne (see page 169), or how to line different pans with parchment for baking (see page 221). Take note, and your cooking experience will be easier and so much more enjoyable.

GATHER-AROUND DINNERS

As I began to write this book, I asked my brother Landon what I should include. He said, "Just tell me what to make. I don't want to think about side dishes or what goes with what. I just want to know what to make, and I'll cook it."

For all of you who have felt the same, this entire chapter is in your honor! Whether you're cooking for a Sunday family gathering, a BBQ, a taco night with friends, or a special holiday like Thanksgiving, I am sharing menus and the most delicious recipes for each complete meal so you don't have to stress about planning.

HOW TO USE THIS CHAPTER

Choose a menu, then follow the recipes. You may need to flip to other chapters to get all the components, but the entire menu is here in the pages of this book.

There is no need to stay true to the menus. Use them as is or as a guide. Feel free to add your own recipes to the mix. The menus I've created have a variety of side dishes and complementary flavors, but they can be great with your own additions too.

mezze dinner

Harissa Tomato Confit | 7

Baba Ghanoush with Pickled Onion and Pomegranate | 8

Crispy Falafel Chickpeas | 10

Labneh with Spice | 10

Cashew Hummus with Lemon-Marinated Mushrooms | 11

Za'atar Cauliflower with Golden Raisins | 13

Jeweled Quinoa Salad | 15

Super-Soft Pita Bread | 16

Sweet and Savory Stuffed Dates | 19

mezze dinner

One of my favorite ways to feed friends and family is to have a glorious array of small dishes from which everyone can create their own meal. This style of dining, called *mezze*, finds its origins in the Mediterranean and Middle East. Like Spanish tapas, this collection of small plates is meant to stimulate your appetite! Mezze spreads are all about ease and letting everyone eat what they want, and the spread can make up an entire meal with its appealing mélange of flavors and textures.

Serve all of the following recipes hot or cold, mixed and matched, and with store-bought sides of olives, pickles, nuts, and sweets, like baklava or honey pastries. Buy a variety of flatbreads and crackers to go with these dishes, or make your own flatbread with my recipe for super-soft pita bread. For a more substantial meal, add main courses such as grilled meats, kebabs, and fish.

A SEASONAL FAVORITE

I serve a mezze meal every chance I get, but I particularly love serving this meal on Christmas Eve. For me, it's a lovely way to bring some flavors from Bethlehem to the table. This kind of menu also allows for the family and friends coming in and out of the house at the holidays.

harissa tomato confit

SERVED HOT OR AT ROOM TEMPERATURE, this confit (vegetables slowly cooked in olive oil) is delicious with Super-Soft Pita Bread (page 16) and Labneh with Spice (page 10), alongside other mezze dishes. You can toss it with couscous, spoon it on a sandwich or slices of baguette, use it to top grilled and roasted meat, or add it to grilled vegetables to create your own recipes and meals.

My tomato confit has a spoonful of spicy harissa for heat and depth of flavor, but it's not too hot. It can be a luscious side, spread, dip, sauce—all of the above!

1½ pints (about 3 cups) cherry tomatoes

2 cloves garlic, sliced

6 sprigs thyme or rosemary

2 to 3 tablespoons harissa

1 teaspoon kosher salt

⅓ cup olive oil

1. Heat oven to 325°F. Combine all ingredients in a 9-inch round or oval baking dish. Bake until flavors meld and tomatoes are very soft, stirring once or twice, 45 to 55 minutes.

2. Cool slightly before serving. Confit may be served warm or at room temperature and can be refrigerated for up to a week; reheat to serve.

SERVES

6 TO 8

MAKES

2 CUPS

HANDS-ON TIME

10 MINUTES

TOTAL TIME

1 HOUR

TARA'S TIP

If you have a pretty baking dish or casserole pan, serve it right out of that dish at the table. You can divide the mixture between a few smaller dishes as well and have several on the buffet or table.

NOTE Use any herbs you have: sage, rosemary, oregano, and thyme are all lovely options.

Harissa is a chili paste that can range from very hot to mild. It's made from dried chili peppers that have been rehydrated and blended with olive oil, spices, and sometimes vinegar and fresh peppers. Harissa flavor varies and can be smoky, tangy, saucy, or thick. Any variation will work in this recipe; adjust the amount you use depending on the taste or heat.

SERVES

6 TO 8

MAKES

ABOUT 3 CUPS

HANDS-ON TIME

35 MINUTES

TOTAL TIME

1 HOUR 10 MINUTES

TARA'S TIP

If you don't have a gas burner stove, you can broil the eggplants close to the broiling element in the oven to char the skin, or cook it on an outdoor grill as close to the flame as possible.

baba ghanoush with pickled onion and pomegranate

THE ORIGIN OF BABA GHANOUSH is claimed by nearly every country in the Middle East, and each one insists on a variation of spice or preparation. I'm adding my twist by topping a classic tahini and garlic version with tangy onions and juicy pomegranates.

I love the smoky flavor in this dip. It's crucial to really blacken the skin of the eggplant for that smoky flavor; that char makes this dish authentic.

BABA GHANOUSH

2 eggplants (about 2 pounds)

⅓ cup tahini

2 large cloves garlic

1 tablespoon fresh lemon juice

¼ teaspoon ground cumin, plus more for garnish

2 tablespoons olive oil

1½ teaspoons kosher salt

Pomegranate arils for garnish

SPICED PICKLED ONIONS

1 medium red onion

2 tablespoons red wine vinegar

¼ teaspoon kosher salt

⅛ teaspoon ground cumin

⅛ teaspoon cayenne pepper

⅛ teaspoon ground coriander

1. For the baba ghanoush: Heat oven to 400°F. Line a baking sheet with foil and set aside.
2. Char eggplants by cooking them directly over the flame on a gas stove, turning occasionally, until the outside is charred and black, 10 to 15 minutes.
3. Transfer eggplants to prepared baking sheet and roast in the oven until they are very tender, 25 to 35 minutes.
4. For the onions: While eggplant roasts, peel onion and cut, from root to tip, into ½-inch wedges.
5. Toss onion with vinegar, salt, and spices. Let sit for 30 minutes before serving. Onion can be refrigerated for up to a day.
6. In the bowl of a food processor, blend tahini, garlic, lemon juice, cumin, olive oil, and salt.
7. When eggplants are cool enough to handle, discard skin and stems and spoon all the flesh into the food processor. Pulse, stopping to scrape down sides of bowl, until eggplant is almost completely puréed.
8. Garnish with pickled onion and pomegranate arils and serve. Sprinkle with extra cumin if desired.

crispy falafel chickpeas

MAKES

1½ CUPS

HANDS-ON TIME

25 MINUTES

TOTAL TIME

1 HOUR

CRISPY CHICKPEAS don't last long at my house. Before they land on a salad, as a topper for a dip, or sprinkled onto soup, they have been eaten out of hand as a crunchy snack. These tasty oven-baked beans can even be sprinkled on your veggie side dishes.

Whatever spice mixture or seasoning you use, the method for making them is the same, so please experiment. I've made these with all the delicious seasonings you'd find in falafel, so not only are they perfect as a snack, but they also work as a topper for hummus, for labneh dips, and on my mezze spread.

Pictured on page 6 with the TOMATO CONFIT.

TARA'S TIP

Repeat rubbing the chickpeas in the towel once or twice to remove more skins; it just take a few minutes. It's not necessary to remove all the skins, but it is nice because the skins may get unpleasantly charred in the oven.

2 (15-ounce) cans chickpeas	½ teaspoon ground cumin
2 tablespoons olive oil	¼ teaspoon ground black pepper
1 teaspoon dried parsley	¼ teaspoon chili powder
1 teaspoon ground coriander	¼ teaspoon garlic powder
½ teaspoon kosher salt	

1. Heat oven to 375°F. Line a baking sheet with parchment and set aside.
2. Rinse and drain chickpeas, shaking off as much water as possible. Place them on a clean towel or paper towels and pat gently to dry. Place another towel on top, then rub the chickpeas and remove as many of the chickpea skins as possible.
3. In a medium bowl, combine chickpeas with olive oil and spices.
4. Pour chickpeas onto prepared baking sheet and spread them into a single layer. Bake until crispy and dry, 45 to 50 minutes, shaking the pan gently to move them around a few times while cooking. Cook until the chickpeas are browned but before they become very dark and hard. They will crisp more as they cool.
5. Serve, or store cooled chickpeas in an airtight container for up to 1 week.

labneh with spice

SERVES

8 TO 10

MAKES

2 CUPS

TOTAL TIME

5 MINUTES

LABNEH IS STRAINED YOGURT so creamy and thick it is called a cheese in the Middle East. You can substitute plain full-fat yogurt for the labneh or even strain your own Greek yogurt. This creamy, slightly tangy dip for veggies, pita, and meats is made even better with spices and a generous drizzle of olive oil.

Pictured on page 9 with the BABA GHANOUSH.

2 cups labneh or plain full-fat yogurt	½ teaspoon ground cumin
¼ cup extra-virgin olive oil	1 teaspoon ground coriander
2 teaspoons toasted sesame seeds	Assorted olives for serving

1. Spread labneh on a platter in a ¾-inch layer. Drizzle with olive oil and sprinkle with sesame seeds, cumin, and coriander.
2. Serve with olives alongside other mezze dishes.

cashew hummus with lemon-marinated mushrooms

FOR THIS HUMMUS, I recommend recooking the canned chickpeas with baking soda. It softens the chickpea skins through a chemical reaction, which results in an ultra-smooth hummus without much effort.

I swapped traditional tahini for creamy cashew butter for a unique, mild flavor, then topped the dip with charred mushrooms marinated in lemon and spice.

Pictured on page 9 with the BABA GHANOUSH.

SERVES

6 TO 8

MAKES

3½ CUPS

HANDS-ON TIME

35 MINUTES

TOTAL TIME

1 HOUR 35 MINUTES

MUSHROOM MARINADE

- ½ teaspoon kosher salt
- Lemon peel from half a lemon (about 4 strips)
- 2 teaspoons fresh lemon juice
- ⅓ cup extra-virgin olive oil
- ¼ teaspoon red pepper flakes
- 2 garlic cloves, smashed
- 1 teaspoon chopped thyme
- 1 teaspoon chopped oregano
- 10 ounces mixed mushrooms (cremini, button, shiitake), sliced or quartered

HUMMUS

- 2 (15-ounce) cans chickpeas
- 1 teaspoon baking soda
- ⅓ cup fresh lemon juice
- 3 cloves garlic
- ½ teaspoon ground cumin
- 1½ teaspoons kosher salt
- ½ cup cashew butter
- Hot water
- Olive oil for drizzling (optional)

TARA'S TIP

Use a vegetable peeler to get the lemon peel for the marinade.

If you don't have a cast-iron skillet, you can char the mushrooms in a standard skillet.

1. For the mushroom marinade: In an 8- or 9-inch round baking dish, vigorously rub salt on the lemon peel with your fingers. Add lemon juice, olive oil, red pepper flakes, garlic, thyme, and oregano to create marinade. Set aside.

2. Heat a cast-iron skillet over medium-high heat for 2 to 3 minutes. Add mushrooms and let them char, stirring only occasionally, until parts are blackened, about 5 minutes. Add mushrooms to marinade and stir to coat. Cover and marinate 1 to 2 hours at room temperature.

3. For the hummus: In a large saucepan, cover chickpeas and their canned liquid with ½ inch water. Add baking soda and bring to a boil, then immediately reduce heat so the mixture doesn't boil over. Simmer until chickpeas are very soft, about 5 minutes. Drain and rinse in hot water in a colander.

4. While chickpeas boil, in a food processor combine lemon juice, garlic, cumin, salt, and cashew butter. Pulse a few times to combine.

5. When chickpeas are ready, add hot chickpeas to the food processor and blend until smooth, scraping the bowl as needed. Drizzle in a few tablespoons of hot water, one at a time, until desired creamy consistency is achieved.

6. Serve hummus in a bowl or on a platter topped with marinated mushrooms and marinade. Hummus may be served warm or at room temperature. Use extra olive oil if desired. Hummus can be refrigerated for up to a week.

za'atar cauliflower with golden raisins

SERVES

6 TO 8

MAKES

ABOUT 6 CUPS

HANDS-ON TIME

10 MINUTES

TOTAL TIME

35 MINUTES

THIS EASY VEGGIE SIDE is lovely served hot or at room temperature, which makes it perfect for a buffet or mezze spread. The golden raisins and Middle Eastern spice mixture create a sweet-and-savory taste that goes well with a variety of other sides and mains at any meal.

Za'atar is a blend of savory dried herbs and spices including sumac, sesame seeds, and often thyme and oregano. Each brand or recipe will be slightly different in flavor. Za'atar is also great added to a dish of olive oil for dipping Super-Soft Pita Bread (page 16) into.

1½ heads cauliflower (8 cups florets)

1 teaspoon za'atar spice, plus more for serving

½ teaspoon kosher salt

3 tablespoons olive oil

⅓ cup golden raisins

1. Heat oven to 400°F. Cut cauliflower into approximately 2-inch florets; you will have about 8 cups of florets.
2. In a large bowl, combine za'atar, salt, and olive oil. Add cauliflower and toss to coat. Spread on a rimmed baking sheet.
3. Roast florets until parts are golden brown, 25 to 30 minutes, turning with a spatula halfway through.
4. Sprinkle with golden raisins and extra za'atar to serve.

NOTE Make this recipe even easier by purchasing pre-cut cauliflower florets where available. You'll need 8 cups, which is about 2½ pounds.

jeweled quinoa salad

NOT ONLY DOES this grain salad look gorgeous with all the colorful veggies and fruit, but the flavors are fresh and bright and delightfully sweet and savory. I could make an entire meal of this salad, my Labneh with Spice (page 10), and my Super-Soft Pita Bread (page 16). But this salad is good as a side for any meal. Serve with meat main dishes, as part of a vegetarian meal, or in a Mediterranean spread like I do.

SERVES

6 TO 8

MAKES

4 CUPS

HANDS-ON TIME

20 MINUTES

TOTAL TIME

50 MINUTES

1⅓ cups water

⅔ cup (4.5 ounces) uncooked quinoa

Pinch salt

¾ cup finely diced red bell pepper

¼ cup finely diced red onion

⅓ cup (2 ounces) walnuts, coarsely chopped

⅓ cup dried cranberries

⅓ cup golden raisins

¼ cup chopped flat-leaf parsley

¼ cup chopped cilantro

¼ cup extra-virgin olive oil

¼ cup fresh lemon juice

Kosher salt to taste

1. In a medium saucepan over high heat, bring water to a boil. Add quinoa and salt and return to a boil. Cover and reduce heat to medium. Cook until water is absorbed, about 10 minutes. Let cool completely.

2. Once quinoa is cool, mix with all remaining ingredients. Salad can be made up to a day in advance. Keep refrigerated.

MAKES

10 PITAS

WORK TIME

25 MINUTES

TOTAL TIME

1 HOUR 50 MINUTES

super-soft pita bread

THIS HOMEMADE PITA BREAD is so much better than store-bought! It's just like the lofty, puffy pitas served at my neighborhood Israeli restaurant. I am known to dream about them occasionally!

The yogurt adds flavor as well as acid and milk solids, which help create the soft texture. These pitas are just as delicious plain as with toppings or dip.

¾ cup warm water

3 tablespoons olive oil, plus more for the bowl

¾ cup whole-milk Greek yogurt

1 package (2¼ teaspoons) active dry yeast

1 teaspoon plus 1 tablespoon granulated sugar

3 cups all-purpose flour (384 g), plus more for dusting

1½ teaspoons fine salt

1. In a large mixing bowl or the bowl of a stand mixer, combine water, olive oil, and yogurt. Add yeast, sugar, flour, and salt, and mix with a wooden spoon or dough hook to combine.

2. Knead either in the stand mixer with the dough hook attachment or on a clean work surface, adding more flour if needed, until dough is soft and slightly sticky (4 to 5 minutes in a mixer, 7 to 10 minutes by hand).

3. Transfer dough to an oiled bowl, cover with a towel or plastic wrap, and let rise until doubled in size, 45 to 50 minutes.

4. Turn dough out onto a clean work surface and divide into 10 equal balls, almost 3 ounces each. Cover and let rise an additional 20 minutes.

5. Meanwhile, heat oven to 475°F with the rack in the lower third. Line two baking sheets with parchment.

6. On a floured work surface, roll balls into circles that are 7 inches in diameter and ⅛-inch thick (or 5-inch circles ¼-inch thick for mini pitas). Place on baking sheets an inch apart.

7. Bake, one sheet at a time, until puffy and lightly browned on top. Begin checking at 5 minutes. I bake them for 7 to 8 minutes, rotating the pan after 5 minutes if one side of the sheet is puffing up more than the other.

8. Transfer pitas to a wire rack to cool. Serve or cool and store in an airtight container up to a day. To warm pitas, wrap in foil and place in a 325°F oven for 10 to 15 minutes.

sweet and savory stuffed dates

DATES ALWAYS MAKE an appearance on Muslim tables during Ramadan (the holy Islamic month of fasting), both at the beginning of the meal and at the end. The tradition is to eat a date at the beginning of the evening meal—after fasting during daylight hours—to give you a burst of energy for the feast to come. At the end of the feast, stuffed dates are served as a sweet dessert along with other nibbles and pastries.

These sweet and savory dates are wonderful on a Mediterranean meal spread. Offer them alongside dips and sides so they can be eaten during or after the meal. Pick your favorite combination or make them all.

WALNUT, ORANGE, AND MANCHEGO STUFFED DATES

- 8 Medjool dates, pitted
- 8 walnut halves
- Zest of half an orange
- ½ teaspoon chopped oregano, plus more for garnish
- Pinch kosher salt
- Shaved Manchego cheese

FENNEL, GOAT CHEESE, AND ALMOND DATES

- 8 Medjool dates, pitted
- 2 ounces soft goat cheese
- ½ teaspoon fennel seeds, finely crushed
- 1 tablespoon honey
- Marcona almonds

MOROCCAN HARISSA AND PISTACHIO DATES

- 8 Medjool dates, pitted
- 2 ounces cream cheese
- 1 heaping tablespoon harissa
- ¼ cup finely ground pistachios

1. For Walnut, Orange, and Manchego Stuffed Dates: Toss walnuts with orange zest, oregano, and salt. Place a shaving of Manchego cheese inside each date along with walnuts. Garnish with extra shavings of cheese and extra oregano.
2. For Fennel, Goat Cheese, and Almond Dates: Blend goat cheese, fennel, and honey together. Transfer to a piping bag or a zip-top bag with a small hole cut in one corner. Pipe cheese inside dates, dividing evenly. Garnish with almonds.
3. For Moroccan Harissa and Pistachio Dates: Blend cream cheese and harissa together. Transfer to a piping bag or a zip-top bag with a small hole cut in one corner. Pipe cheese inside dates, dividing evenly. Dip in ground pistachios.

NOTE Medjool dates are typically large and soft. If your dates are small or vary in size, just use extra filling to make more. You can also use a pairing knife to make a larger opening for the filling if needed.

SERVES

6 TO 8 PER RECIPE

MAKES

8 LARGE DATES PER RECIPE

TOTAL TIME

25 MINUTES

holiday dinner

The holidays are full of food traditions, and whether elaborate or simple and homey, these meals are the memories we take with us through the next year. Cooking together, sharing a beautiful meal, and having that moment for great conversation and connection are priceless.

If a roast turkey in half the time doesn't sell you, then a fresh take on cranberry sauce or the world's most perfect sausage stuffing will! Whether you're sprucing up your grandmother's old Thanksgiving menu, starting your own traditions, or adding a new dish to Christmas dinner, the recipes here are perfect for mixing and matching with your favorites. Or make the entire meal as is—it's truly a glorious combination of all the savory goodness the season has to offer.

classic turkey in pieces

SERVES

10 TO 12

HANDS-ON TIME

35 MINUTES

TOTAL TIME

2 HOURS
15 MINUTES

YOU'LL NEVER GO BACK to cooking a whole bird after making this recipe. I've broken the turkey into its primal cuts, which allows the meat to cook more evenly—in half the time! The meat turns out perfectly cooked, classically flavored, golden brown, and delicious every time—with far less babysitting than a whole turkey. This method frees up the oven sooner, plus the carcass can be simmering into stock for the gravy ahead of time.

I've used my spice cupboard staples for the seasonings so the drippings make tasty gravy, and all you'll need is a standard half-sheet pan and a metal rack that fits inside it.

TARA'S TIP

For turkeys larger than 14 pounds, you will want to use two sheet pans, and I recommend double ovens!

2 ribs celery, roughly chopped

1 medium onion, sliced

1 (12-to-14-pound) turkey, cut into 5 pieces (see Tara's Tip)

6 sprigs herbs (thyme, sage, parsley)

2 cups turkey or chicken stock

2 tablespoons Worcestershire sauce

2 tablespoons light brown sugar, divided

2 teaspoons ground black pepper

1 tablespoon garlic powder

1 tablespoon onion powder

1 tablespoon ground coriander

¾ teaspoon paprika

3 tablespoons kosher salt

5 tablespoons canola or avocado oil

1. Heat oven to 425°F. Spread celery and onion on a rimmed half-sheet pan and set a metal cooling rack over the top. Arrange turkey pieces on the rack with the herbs. Pat turkey dry with a paper towel.

2. Whisk together stock, Worcestershire sauce, and 1 tablespoon brown sugar. Set aside.

3. Mix together remaining tablespoon brown sugar, pepper, garlic powder, onion powder, ground coriander, paprika, salt, and oil. Rub mixture all over turkey, on the skin side and the underside. (You may not use it all.)

4. Place pan in oven and pour 1 cup stock mixture into the baking sheet.

5. Roast turkey, rotating baking sheet halfway through, until skin is light golden brown, about 30 minutes.

6. Reduce oven to 325°F. Baste turkey with broth mixture and continue to roast for 50 to 70 minutes more. Baste

You can cut the turkey in 5 pieces yourself or have the butcher do it (which I recommend): breast, legs (drumsticks and thighs), and wings. (Show the butcher this picture as reference.) Ask for the neck, backbone, wing tips, and giblets along with a few extra wings for making stock. Plan ahead so you can ensure the butcher can thaw a frozen turkey in time.

Continued on next page

GATHER-AROUND DINNERS

25

with broth mixture every 15 to 20 minutes. Add more broth ½ cup at a time to the baking sheet as needed to maintain some liquid at all times. Turkey will cook a total of 1 to 1½ hours, and skin should be a rich golden brown. (Cover with foil if skin starts to get too dark.) Check the temperature of each piece after 1 hour. The internal temperature of each piece should be 160°F to 165°F on an instant-read thermometer. Wings and legs will be done first, after 60 to 80 minutes, and can be removed when done. The breast may take the entire 90 minutes.

7. Transfer turkey pieces to a cutting board and tent with foil for 20 to 30 minutes before carving. (Internal temperature will increase to the required 165°F.)

8. Remove rack from baking sheet and scrape the drippings into a gravy separator to capture the liquid. Discard the solids. Reserve strained liquid for gravy.

9. Carve turkey as desired and arrange on a serving platter.

turkey stock and gravy

I LIKE TO MAKE the stock the day before so it's ready to prepare the gravy the day of. Cut the turkey into parts and brown the carcass, neck, giblets, and wing tips in the oven for extra flavor and to make your stock. I prefer an Instant Pot for ease, but you can simmer the stock in a large, covered pot on the stove for 2 to 3 hours for the same result.

MAKES

2½ QUARTS STOCK
AND 3½ CUPS
GRAVY

HANDS-ON TIME

25 MINUTES

TOTAL TIME

3 HOURS
30 MINUTES

STOCK

3 ribs celery

2 carrots, washed and peeled

1 large onion, washed and peeled

1 turkey carcass, including neck and wing tips (see Tara's Tip on page 25)

2½ quarts plus ½ cup water, divided

1 bunch fresh herbs (such as parsley, sage, and thyme)

2 bay leaves

1 tablespoon peppercorns

GRAVY

Strained drippings from roast turkey, if any (see page 26)

3 cups turkey stock (as prepared on this page)

¼ cup cornstarch

½ cup cold water

1 tablespoon Worcestershire sauce

½ teaspoon fresh or dried thyme

1 teaspoon Better Than Bouillon, chicken or turkey flavor (optional)

Kosher salt to taste

> **TARA'S TIP**
>
> Browning the carcass and veggies adds flavor and color to the turkey stock, but if you are short on time, you can skip this step and add everything raw.

1. For stock: Roughly chop celery and carrots. Cut onion into wedges, with or without the skin.

2. Heat oven to 375°F. Arrange cut vegetables in the bottom of a roasting pan and place the turkey pieces on top. Add ½ cup water and roast until turkey and vegetables are just browning, about 40 minutes.

3. Transfer everything to a 6-to-8-quart Instant Pot or multi-cooker. Add herbs, bay leaves, peppercorns, and remaining 2½ quarts cold water. Seal lid and set on high pressure for 1 hour 30 minutes (90 minutes) or on the soup/broth setting. After cooking, let pressure naturally release for 10 minutes.

4. While pressure releases, prepare an ice bath by filling a bowl with lots of ice and water. Bowl should be large enough to hold the pot insert.

5. Once pressure is released, carefully remove large pieces of bone, meat, and vegetables with tongs and a slotted spoon, and discard. Place pot insert in ice bath and stir occasionally until broth is cool, about 30 minutes.

6. Pour cooled broth through a fine-mesh strainer into jars or containers to store.

7. For gravy: Pour any strained drippings from a roasted turkey into a medium saucepan. Add turkey stock. In a separate bowl, stir together cornstarch and cold water, then whisk cornstarch mixture into pan. Whisking constantly, bring mixture to a boil, then reduce heat to a simmer.

8. Add Worcestershire sauce, thyme, Better Than Bouillon, and salt to taste. Stir and let simmer until thickened. Serve.

silky-soft dinner rolls

THESE LITTLE ROLLS are luxuriously soft. I use a milk-bread technique called *tang-zhong* that makes the rolls so silky, like the bread you find at Chinese and other Asian-style bakeries. The tangzhong starter—a mixture of flour, water, and milk—takes only a few extra minutes of planning ahead and helps the dough retain moisture.

MAKES

25 ROLLS

HANDS-ON TIME

50 MINUTES

TOTAL TIME

2 HOURS
10 MINUTES

TANGZHONG STARTER

½ cup water

½ cup whole milk

6 tablespoons all-purpose flour

ROLLS

4½ to 4¾ cups (576 g) all-purpose flour

1¾ teaspoons fine salt

1 tablespoon plus ½ teaspoon instant yeast

2 tablespoons nonfat dry milk

¾ cup whole milk, warmed

2 large eggs, room temperature

6 tablespoons unsalted butter, softened, plus extra for brushing

Canola or avocado oil for work surface

¼ cup chopped mixed herbs (such as rosemary, parsley, oregano, and thyme) for garnish

> **TARA'S TIP**
>
> This recipe benefits from weighing the flour in the dough, as described on page x in the Introduction. You can also use your scale to weigh each ball of dough to create uniform rolls.
>
> Bake a big pan of rolls or bake in several smaller pans.

1. For tangzhong: In a small saucepan over medium heat, whisk together water, milk, and flour. Cook 2 to 3 minutes, stirring, to thicken. Transfer to a covered bowl and refrigerate until cool.

2. For dough: In the bowl of an electric mixer fitted with the dough hook, combine the 4½ cups (576 g) flour, salt, instant yeast, and dry milk. In a separate bowl, whisk together warm milk, eggs, and cooled tangzhong paste.

3. Add liquid ingredients to dry ingredients in the mixer. Mix on medium speed until combined. Dough will be dry. Add butter a tablespoon at a time as the mixer is going. After the butter is incorporated, knead on medium speed for 6 minutes. Cover bowl with a clean towel and let rest 20 minutes.

4. After 20 minutes, knead the dough again on medium-high speed for 6 more minutes until a smooth dough forms. Add a few tablespoons extra flour as the dough is mixing if it is really sticky. Dough should be soft and smooth.

5. Remove dough hook and use a rubber scraper to bring dough together into a ball. Spray dough and inside of bowl with cooking spray. Cover and transfer to a warm place to proof. Let rise until almost doubled in size and until finger imprint remains and doesn't bounce back when touched, 35 to 45 minutes.

6. Prepare high-sided pans by spraying with cooking spray or brushing with butter.

7. Turn dough out onto an oiled work surface. Measure and weigh into 1½- to 2-ounce pieces. (I made 25 [1.8-ounce] rolls.) Gently roll into tight balls. Arrange ¼- to ½-inch apart in pans. Cover and let rise again until almost doubled in size and until a finger imprint remains on the side when touched, 30 to 40 minutes.

8. While rolls rise, heat oven to 350°F. Once rolls have risen, bake until just golden, 15 to 18 minutes. Brush tops with extra butter and sprinkle with chopped herbs.

Sweet Potatoes
Brussels Sprouts
Mashed Potatoes
Butter
Stuffing
Rolls
Turkey
Cranberry Sauce

GET SET!

Choose, clean, and label your serving dishes the night before hosting dinner. It will help you avoid that last-minute scramble when the food is ready.

fresh orange cranberry sauce

SERVES

10 TO 12

MAKES

2¾ CUPS

HANDS-ON TIME

15 MINUTES

TOTAL TIME

3 HOURS
15 MINUTES OR
OVERNIGHT

THIS SWEET AND TANGY accompaniment to turkey at Thanksgiving is quintessential. I guarantee you'll feel inclined to make a switch from your old cooked standby when you taste this fresh cranberry sauce.

This sauce isn't cloyingly sugary or sticky; it has the right balance of sweet oranges, apple, and crunchy pecans. A hint of spice makes it perfect for any fall meal, and it's even better when made ahead!

2 cups (8 ounces) fresh or frozen cranberries

1 Granny Smith apple, peeled, cored, and quartered

Zest from half an orange

1 navel orange

½ cup granulated sugar

¼ cup finely chopped pecans

1 pinch allspice

1. In a food processor, pulse cranberries and apple until coarsely chopped. Transfer to a medium bowl, and add orange zest.

2. Supreme the segments of the orange. (Cut off the peel and remove the segments from the membrane.) Coarsely chop segments and add to the bowl, then squeeze any juice from membrane into bowl.

3. Add sugar, pecans, and allspice to cranberry-apple mixture. Stir until combined.

4. Cover and refrigerate 3 hours or overnight. Serve chilled. Leftovers can be chilled up to 4 days.

NOTE Leftover sauce is great on a turkey sandwich or on crackers with soft cheese for any holiday snack board.

SERVES

10 TO 12

MAKES

ABOUT 10 CUPS

HANDS-ON TIME

15 MINUTES

TOTAL TIME

45 MINUTES

smoked gouda and scallion mashed potatoes

THIS IS THE ULTIMATE mashed potato side dish, with just a hint of smoky cheese and savory onion. I've used the smoked Gouda cheese sparingly so it's not overpowering, but it truly makes these potatoes great. These mashers are fantastic on their own; with an extra pat of butter; with Thanksgiving turkey gravy; on the side of my Pot Roast (page 61), grilled steak, or chicken; and with Easter ham. Consider halving the recipe for a smaller, weeknight meal.

5 pounds russet potatoes, peeled and cut into 2-inch pieces

4 teaspoons kosher salt, divided

¾ cup whole milk, warmed

2 tablespoons unsalted butter, room temperature

¾ cup (4 ounces) grated smoked Gouda cheese

2 scallions, thinly sliced, divided

1. Place potatoes and 2 teaspoons salt in a large pot. Cover with cold water by 2 inches. Bring to a boil. Reduce heat to a simmer and cook until fork-tender but not falling apart, 25 to 30 minutes. Drain in a colander.

2. Rice the potatoes with a ricer, or transfer them to the bowl of a stand mixer or large bowl. With the stand mixer or an electric mixer fitted with the whisk attachment, beat potatoes on medium speed until finely crumbled. Add remaining 2 teaspoons salt, warm milk, butter, smoked Gouda, and half the scallions. Beat until just smooth, adding more milk if needed for a light, creamy texture.

3. Serve hot. Garnish with remaining scallions and butter if desired.

TARA'S TIP

I used my classic mashed potato recipe here but reduced the butter because of the added cheese. If you are hankering for plain potatoes, use 5 tablespoons of butter instead of 2 and leave out the cheese and scallions. Either way, this method makes perfectly fluffy, delicious spuds.

spicy maple sweet potatoes with cinnamon pepitas

THESE SPICED, GLAZED sweet potatoes are perfect for a fall gathering or Thanksgiving dinner and can be prepped ahead of time and reheated.

For this stovetop side dish, any type of sweet potato or yam will work, as would butternut or Hubbard squash. I added some spice and heat to the maple butter to bring in a bit of sophistication. Then I skipped toasty marshmallows as the sweet-potato topping and added crunchy, candied pepitas instead. If you don't have pepitas, you can sub another nut to the spicy, candied topping. This side dish is glorious!

SERVES

6 TO 8

HANDS-ON TIME

30 MINUTES

TOTAL TIME

50 MINUTES

PEPITAS

¼ cup pure maple syrup

¼ teaspoon cinnamon

⅛ teaspoon cayenne pepper

½ cup pepitas (hulled pumpkin seeds)

SWEET POTATOES

4 medium sweet potatoes (about 2½ pounds)

3 tablespoons olive or avocado oil

¼ cup finely diced shallot or red onion

1 teaspoon kosher salt

⅔ cup chicken or vegetable broth

¼ teaspoon sweet paprika

⅛ teaspoon cinnamon

⅛ teaspoon cayenne pepper

¼ teaspoon garlic powder

3 tablespoons pure maple syrup

2 tablespoons butter

> **TARA'S TIP**
>
> To prep ahead, make the pepitas and keep in an airtight container. Peel, cut, and cook the sweet potatoes through step 6. Cool and store cooked potatoes in the fridge for up to 2 days. When ready to serve, heat potatoes in a covered nonstick skillet until warmed through, then continue with step 7.

1. For pepitas: Line a baking sheet with parchment or a silicone baking mat. Set aside.

2. In a small saucepan or skillet, combine maple syrup, cinnamon, and cayenne over medium-high heat. Bring to a boil and add pepitas. Boil, stirring constantly, until maple syrup is almost gone and mixture is thick and getting darker in color, 3 to 4 minutes.

3. Remove from heat and pour glazed pepitas on prepared baking sheet. Working quickly, spread the seeds out in a single layer using a spatula or forks. Let cool completely, then break or chop into small clusters.

4. For sweet potatoes: Peel potatoes and cut into 1-inch pieces.

5. In a large nonstick skillet with a lid, heat oil over medium-high heat. Add sweet potatoes, shallot, and salt and stir to coat with oil. Reduce heat to medium. Cook sweet potatoes, stirring occasionally, until they soften, about 5 minutes.

6. Add broth and cover skillet. Reduce heat to medium-low and let sweet potatoes cook until tender but not falling apart, 12 to 14 minutes.

7. Remove lid and add spices and maple syrup. Gently stir to allow syrup to bubble and glaze potatoes for 1 minute. Add butter and stir to coat. Remove from heat.

8. Serve sweet potatoes while they are still warm, topped with candied pepitas.

GATHER-AROUND DINNERS

35

favorite sausage stuffing

IT HAS TAKEN YEARS, and I mean years, to make a stuffing my entire family agrees on. One person likes sausage, someone else likes the bread cubes a certain size, I like a little sweetness (cue dried apricots and apples), and the herbs and seasonings must taste like grandma's (without anyone ever having grandma's recipe!). Every Thanksgiving, we add a pinch of this, try a cup of that, fiddle with the flavors, vary the amount of butter or broth. I finally made the ultimate stuffing, and it was a hit.

Don't skip on the mix of dry and fresh herbs and spices; it's really the golden ticket to the success of this dish.

You can prepare the stuffing a day in advance, and the recipe is easily divided in half for a smaller crowd, but just know: leftovers are delicious!

SERVES

10 TO 12

MAKES

ABOUT 13 CUPS

HANDS-ON TIME

35 MINUTES

TOTAL TIME

1 HOUR 20 MINUTES

1 pound day-old sourdough or French bread

1 pound sweet Italian sausage, casing removed

1 tablespoon olive oil

½ cup butter, divided

3 cups finely chopped yellow onion

2 cups finely diced celery

½ cup chopped dried apricots

¾ cup finely chopped flat-leaf parsley

1 tablespoon chopped fresh thyme

1½ tablespoons chopped fresh sage

1 tablespoon dry mustard powder

1 tablespoon ground coriander

1 teaspoon celery seed

1 teaspoon dried basil

¼ teaspoon turmeric

½ teaspoon garlic powder

½ teaspoon dried rubbed sage

1 teaspoon kosher salt

½ teaspoon ground black pepper

2 cups low-sodium chicken broth

TARA'S TIP

For a classic texture and chewiness to your stuffing, plan ahead: Cut the bread into cubes, spread them out on a baking sheet, cover them with a towel, and let them sit overnight or until completely dried.

1. Cut bread into ¼-to-½-inch cubes and set aside in a large mixing bowl.

2. In a large high-sided skillet or Dutch oven, cook sausage over medium-high heat, breaking it up into very small pieces. Sauté until cooked through and browned, about 5 minutes. Remove from pan and set aside.

3. Add olive oil and ¼ cup butter to pan. Add onion and celery. Reduce heat to medium and cook, stirring occasionally, until soft and translucent, 8 to 10 minutes. Remove from heat and stir in remaining ¼ cup butter until melted.

4. To large mixing bowl with bread cubes, add cooked veggies, cooked sausage, apricots, herbs, and spices. Stir well to coat evenly. Drizzle in broth, stirring between additions to allow all the bread to absorb the liquid.

5. Store stuffing in an airtight container or baking dish in the fridge overnight, or cook immediately.

6. Heat oven to 350°F. Transfer stuffing to one large casserole dish (9-by-13-inches or 3 quarts). Cover with foil and bake until heated through, about 30 minutes. Uncover and cook until top is just crisping and golden brown, 15 minutes more. Serve hot. Leftovers can be refrigerated for up to 5 days.

SERVES

6 TO 8

HANDS-ON TIME

15 MINUTES

TOTAL TIME

50 MINUTES

miso honey brussels sprouts

I FIRST HAD BRUSSELS like these at a Japanese restaurant up the street. They came in a little bowl, and after the first bite, I realized I could eat at least ten servings! They were so good.

I've experimented and perfected the recipe so we can all make it at home. The umami, sweet, and salty flavors go with almost any meal. Pomegranates add a festive flare for a holiday meal, but you can leave them out if you're making this when they aren't in season.

GLAZE

¼ cup honey

1 tablespoon white miso

1 tablespoon lemon juice

¼ teaspoon red pepper flakes

BRUSSELS SPROUTS

1½ pounds Brussels sprouts, trimmed and cleaned, large ones cut in half

2 cloves garlic, minced

½ teaspoon kosher salt

3 tablespoons canola or avocado oil

½ cup walnut pieces

⅓ cup pomegranate arils (optional)

1. Heat oven to 400°F.

2. For glaze: In a small saucepan or in the microwave, heat all glaze ingredients until just hot. Whisk together to combine. Set aside.

3. For Brussels sprouts: In a large bowl or on a rimmed baking sheet, toss Brussels sprouts with garlic, salt, and oil. Spread out on baking sheet.

4. Roast until tender and parts are golden brown and charred, 20 to 25 minutes. During the last 5 minutes of cooking, drizzle Brussels sprouts with glaze and add walnuts. Serve garnished with pomegranate arils.

fiesta mexicana

Blackened Salmon Tacos with Mangoes
and Purple Slaw | 45

Orange Cumin Carnitas | 46

Tacos Carnitas with Pineapple Salsa
and Avocado Cream | 48

Serrano Chili Avocado Cream | 51

Pineapple Taco Topper | 51

Fresh Green Salsa | 52

Spicy El Pato and Mango Blender Salsa | 52

Mexican Red Rice | 53

Tex-Mex Brisket Tacos with El Pato
and Mango Salsa | 55

fiesta mexicana

This gathering menu is a taco fiesta gone wild! From salsas and sauces for any type of taco or chip dip to the perfect Mexican red rice, you'll be glad you got this party started.

Grab your sombrero and choose a blackened salmon taco, Tex-Mex brisket taco, or an easy-to-make Instant Pot carnitas taco! They are great for a feast, or you can pick one for a weeknight dinner with the fam.

I've turned main dishes from other meals into taco fillings, so these tacos are all easy to make the day after you've prepared the meat. In other chapters, you'll also find additional tasty accompaniments, like chili con queso and a loaded guacamole dip, to make this party your own.

blackened salmon tacos with mangoes and purple slaw

SERVES

6 TO 8

MAKES

8 TACOS

TOTAL TIME

15 MINUTES, NOT INCLUDING SALMON PREPARATION

IF YOU'RE HANDY with a knife, you can slice, shave, and julienne the cabbage and radishes. I prefer to use a mandoline. The main slicing blade is great for the cabbage, and I switch to the julienne slicer for the radishes. Of course, use the mandoline guard or a protective glove to keep your fingers safe.

The cotija, a crumbly Mexican cheese, is a nice addition to the tacos, and I like to serve extra on the side for diners to add more.

PURPLE SLAW

1½ cups thinly sliced purple cabbage

1 cup julienned or chopped radishes (about 8 radishes)

¼ teaspoon ground cumin

½ cup crumbled cotija cheese

TACOS

2 tablespoons avocado or canola oil

8 corn tortillas (16 if you like to double wrap the tacos)

Half a recipe Blackened Salmon with Mango-Lime Salsa (page 158)

⅓ cup chopped cilantro

Lime wedges for serving

Hot sauce for serving

Cotija cheese for serving

1. For the purple slaw: Toss together cabbage, radishes, and cumin. Just before serving, add cotija cheese.

2. Brush oil lightly on tortillas. Toast over a flame or panfry in a nonstick skillet over medium heat until just soft. Set tortillas aside either wrapped in a towel or in a warm oven to keep warm if desired.

3. To assemble the tacos, fill tortillas with a bit of purple slaw, then top with some flaked salmon and lime mango salsa. Serve with cilantro, limes for squeezing, hot sauce, and extra cotija on the side.

SERVES

10 TO 12

MAKES

6 CUPS SHREDDED
CARNITAS

HANDS-ON TIME

25 MINUTES

TOTAL TIME

1 HOUR 35 MINUTES

orange cumin carnitas

MY SLOW-COOKED PULLED PORK is meant to be easy and versatile. There are no overpowering flavors here; a sweet orange acidity and some smokiness from adobo (the sauce in a can of chipotles in adobo) balance the garlic and brown sugar. While perfect for Tacos Carnitas (page 48), these carnitas can be used on nachos, in pulled pork sandwiches (with your favorite BBQ sauce), or in enchiladas.

4 pounds boneless pork shoulder or pork butt, fatty rind removed

4 cloves garlic, crushed

2 tablespoons adobo sauce from canned chipotles in adobo

2 tablespoons brown sugar

2 tablespoons white vinegar

2 teaspoons kosher salt

1 teaspoon dried oregano

1 teaspoon ground cumin

1 tablespoon orange zest

Juice of 1 orange

1. Cut pork into fist-sized pieces. In the insert of a 4- to 6-quart Instant Pot, add all ingredients. Stir or turn pork with tongs to coat evenly.
2. Seal and set pressure cooker on high for 40 minutes. Let pressure naturally release for 20 minutes, then manually release the remaining pressure.
3. Remove pork and shred into pieces with two forks. Strain liquid and set aside.
4. If desired, crisp carnitas in the broiler. Heat broiler to high and spread carnitas on a foil-lined rimmed baking sheet. Pour about ½ cup reserved cooking liquid over pork and broil until tips are just crispy, 4 to 5 minutes. Watch closely so the pork doesn't burn.
5. Carnitas can be made in advance and refrigerated up to 3 days. To reheat, add pork and some cooking liquid to a skillet and gently heat.

TARA'S TIP

This recipe is easily doubled using a larger pressure cooker. Freeze leftovers for up to 3 months.

For a slow cooker, combine all ingredients in the crock of a slow cooker, cover, and cook on high for 4 to 5 hours, until pork is very tender and falls apart.

SERVES

6 TO 8

MAKES

8 TACOS

TOTAL TIME

10 MINUTES, NOT
INCLUDING OTHER
RECIPE PREP

tacos carnitas with pineapple salsa and avocado cream

CARNITAS AND PINEAPPLE seem to go together like peas and carrots! With the addition of a creamy, spicy avocado sauce, these tacos are one of my favorite meals. I added jalapeño to the salsa for a little kick, but feel free to serve these with your favorite hot sauce if you want more heat.

8 small flour tortillas

1 recipe Orange Cumin Carnitas
(page 46)

1 recipe Serrano Chili Avocado Cream
(page 51)

1 recipe Pineapple Taco Topper
(page 51)

Lime wedges for serving

1. Heat flour tortillas in a skillet or in the oven.
2. Fill each with about ⅓ cup carnitas and top with avocado cream and Pineapple Taco Topper. Serve with lime wedges for squeezing.

NOTE A full recipe of Orange Cumin Carnitas yields about 16 tacos, so if you are serving a crowd, use the full amount for double the tacos here.

serrano chili avocado cream

A DRIZZLE OF THIS CREAM on a taco is life-changing. It plays the part of both guacamole, with the tang of lime, and a hot sauce, touting a flirtatious amount of serrano chili. You can make this creamy sauce especially for the Tex-Mex Brisket Tacos (page 55) and the Tacos Carnitas (page 48). It is also fantastic on roast chicken, on steak off the grill, as a salad dressing, on a baked potato, and as a dip for tortilla chips or veggies.

MAKES

ABOUT 2 CUPS

TOTAL TIME

15 MINUTES

3 ripe avocados, pitted and scooped from skin

Half a small serrano chili

1 clove garlic

1 scallion, roughly chopped

½ cup roughly chopped cilantro

⅓ cup sour cream or plain Greek yogurt

⅓ cup cold water

¼ cup fresh lime juice

1 teaspoon kosher salt

TARA'S TIP

To serve drizzled, I transfer the cream to a squeeze bottle (or a zip-top bag with the corner snipped off) and squeeze a squiggle onto my tacos.

1. Add everything to a blender and blend until smooth. Season to taste with salt or more lime juice.
2. Serve immediately or store in an airtight container in the fridge for up to 3 days.

pineapple taco topper

FANTASTIC ON ANY taco or as a dip for chips, this salsa is ideal on top of the Tacos Carnitas (page 48).

MAKES

ABOUT 2½ CUPS

HANDS-ON TIME

15 MINUTES

TOTAL TIME

25 MINUTES

2 tablespoons fresh lime juice

1 tablespoon honey

Pinch red pepper flakes

¼ teaspoon kosher salt

1 small jalapeño, seeds removed

¼ of a small red onion

1½ cups diced pineapple

1. In a medium bowl, stir together lime juice, honey, red pepper flakes, and salt.
2. Finely dice the jalapeño and thinly slice the red onion from root to tip. Add to lime mixture.
3. Stir in pineapple and let sit for 10 minutes before serving.
4. Salsa can be made up to 2 hours in advance and stored in the fridge.

fresh green salsa

MAKES

ABOUT 2 CUPS

TOTAL TIME

15 MINUTES

YOU NAME IT, this fresh salsa should be on it! Sprinkle it on tacos, enchiladas, chili, queso dip, or nachos. The list could go on, but you get the idea. It's the perfect combination of green flavors for any fiesta or to spruce up a weeknight dinner.

Pictured on page 50.

1½ cups chopped cilantro

¾ cup finely sliced scallions

⅓ cup finely diced, seeded jalapeño

1. Combine all ingredients and serve. Salsa can be prepped up to 2 hours ahead and stored, covered, in the refrigerator.

NOTE For smaller meals, halve this recipe: ¾ cup chopped cilantro, 6 tablespoons sliced scallions, and 2 to 3 tablespoons diced jalapeño.

spicy el pato and mango blender salsa

MAKES

ABOUT 2¼ CUPS

TOTAL TIME

20 MINUTES

THIS TOMATOEY SALSA is super easy to put together and gets better with age. A day or so in the fridge allows the flavors to combine, but who can wait that long? Dip chips right in or spoon over Tex-Mex Brisket Tacos (page 55).

Pictured on page 50.

1 ripe mango

3 scallions, coarsely chopped

1 cup diced fresh tomatoes

⅓ cup coarsely chopped cilantro

¼ cup canned El Pato sauce

2½ tablespoons fresh lime juice

2 tablespoons finely chopped jalapeño

¾ teaspoon kosher salt

¼ teaspoon black pepper

¼ teaspoon garlic powder

1. Peel and roughly chop mango.
2. Add mango and remaining ingredients to a blender. Blend on medium until almost completely puréed. If you have a very powerful blender, you can pulse the mixture until you get the consistency you desire.
3. Serve immediately or store in the fridge for up to 4 days.

NOTE El Pato sauce is a canned tomato sauce with chilis, onions, garlic, and spices. You'll find it in a yellow can in your grocery store. There isn't a perfect substitute, but if you can't find it, use a small can of traditional tomato sauce with ½ teaspoon ground cumin, ½ teaspoon dried oregano, and several splashes of hot sauce, and then increase the garlic powder in this recipe to ½ teaspoon.

mexican red rice

THIS RICE isn't that flavorless stuff you get with your enchilada at a restaurant; it's the perfect balance of tomatoey tang and savory goodness for any Mexican meal. You'll love how beautifully red and tasty this rice comes out every time you make it.

If you want a touch of extra spice, leave the seeds in the jalapeño when you chop it.

SERVES

6 TO 8

MAKES

5 CUPS

HANDS-ON TIME

15 MINUTES

TOTAL TIME

50 MINUTES

2 tablespoons avocado or canola oil

½ cup finely diced onion

2 tablespoons finely diced, seeded jalapeño

1½ cups long-grain rice

1 cup canned crushed tomatoes

1⅔ cups water

½ teaspoon garlic powder

1 teaspoon kosher salt

Cilantro or Fresh Green Salsa (page 52) for garnish, if desired

1. Add oil to a medium saucepan over medium-high heat. When oil is hot, add onion, jalapeño, and rice. Cook, stirring frequently, until onions are soft and rice is becoming golden in parts, 4 to 5 minutes.

2. Add crushed tomatoes, water, garlic powder, and salt and stir to combine. Bring to a simmer. Reduce heat to low, cover, and cook 15 minutes.

3. Remove from heat and let sit, covered, for 10 more minutes. Remove lid and use a spoon to fluff the rice. Serve hot and garnish with cilantro. Leftover rice can be refrigerated up to a week.

tex-mex brisket tacos with el pato and mango salsa

SLAP ON YOUR COWBOY BOOTS and gingham shirt because you're going to want to be as authentic as these flavor-packed tacos when you dig in! There's a hint of Mexican flare to my smoky, spicy, fruity tacos, and every bite will bring you back for more.

The Texas-Style Beef Brisket (page 155) is really the star, and these tacos are a great way to use any leftover brisket from your weekend BBQ.

SERVES

6 TO 8

MAKES

8 TACOS

TOTAL TIME

25 MINUTES, NOT INCLUDING BRISKET PREP

Half a recipe Texas-Style Beef Brisket (page 155)

Canola or avocado oil

8 corn tortillas

Thinly sliced radishes

Thinly sliced jalapeño

Crumbled cotija cheese

1 recipe Spicy El Pato and Mango Blender Salsa (page 52)

1. If reheating leftover brisket, wrap it in foil and heat in a 350°F oven for about 15 minutes. Shred brisket into small pieces.
2. Brush oil lightly on tortillas. Toast over a flame or panfry in a nonstick skillet over medium heat until just soft. Wrap in foil and keep in a warm oven.
3. To assemble the tacos, fill each tortilla with warm brisket and top with radishes, jalapeño, crumbled cotija, and loads of El Pato mango salsa.

TARA'S TIP

If you have any Texsaucy BBQ Sauce (page 155) leftover from your brisket, toss a little bit of sauce with the shredded brisket before assembling the tacos for a flavorful zing!

sunday supper

Pot Roast with Pearl Onions and Carrots | 61

Creamed Spinach | 62

Sheet Pan Potatoes | 64

Waldorf Salad with Radicchio and
Buttermilk Dressing | 67

Dill Bread | 68

Green Beans with Shallot Dressing | 71

sunday supper

Mom's Sunday pot roast dinner is memorable—slow-cooked beef, always with gravy made from the drippings, and fluffy mashed potatoes. You'd find some kind of tasty veggie on the table, butter and jam for bread or rolls, and either a Jell-O salad (yes, that's right!) or a Waldorf salad with sweetened whipped cream.

I have re-created those delicious memories with an updated flare, and I think you'll want to dig in. Bring your family or friends together on a cozy weekend evening for this noteworthy meal.

pot roast with pearl onions and carrots

SERVES

8 TO 10

MAKES

1 POT ROAST

HANDS-ON TIME

25 MINUTES

TOTAL TIME

4 HOURS

I LIKE USING PEARL ONIONS with a slow-cooked roast because they hold their shape rather than falling apart like sliced onions. They are bite-sized, and they take on the flavors of the entire dish to be melt-in-your-mouth delicious.

Opt for chuck roast when making classic pot roast. It is a well-marbled cut that becomes very tender with long low-heat cooking.

1 (4-to-5-pound) chuck roast

Kosher salt and ground black pepper

2 tablespoons canola or avocado oil

6 carrots, peeled

3 cups (12-to-14-ounce bag) frozen pearl onions

8 ounces cremini mushrooms, cleaned

4 cups beef broth

2 tablespoons honey

3 tablespoons Worcestershire sauce

1 tablespoon balsamic vinegar

Thyme and rosemary sprigs

2 bay leaves

GRAVY

Strained drippings

Up to 1½ cups water or beef broth

2 tablespoons cornstarch

½ cup cold water

Salt

TARA'S TIP

To make this in a slow cooker, follow the first 2 steps, then transfer to a slow cooker. Add remaining ingredients and cook on high for 5 to 6 hours until roast is very tender.

1. Heat oven to 325°F. Tie roast with kitchen twine if not compact or if in two pieces. Season beef on all sides with salt and pepper.

2. Heat oil in a large Dutch oven over medium-high heat. Sear beef on all sides until dark brown, about 10 minutes total. Remove pan from heat.

3. Leave carrots whole, or cut into 2-inch pieces. Add carrots, pearl onions, mushrooms, beef broth, honey, Worcestershire sauce, vinegar, a few sprigs of herbs, and bay leaves to the pan. Cover and roast in oven until beef is fork-tender, 3 to 3½ hours.

4. If desired, you can strain any juices from the cooked roast to make a gravy. Put strained drippings in a saucepan and add water or beef broth to make a total of 1½ cups liquid. Bring to a boil. Whisk cornstarch with ½ cup cold water and stir into the sauce. Mixture will thicken in about 1 minute. Season with salt to taste. Remove from heat and serve with roast.

SERVES

6

MAKES

2½ CUPS

HANDS-ON TIME

25 MINUTES

TOTAL TIME

35 MINUTES

creamed spinach

MY IDEAL CREAMY SPINACH side dish is flavorful and rich, not watery and soupy—so I came up with my own ridiculously delicious recipe. It's a great accompaniment to Sunday pot roast, grilled steak, or baked chicken, and it reheats well for leftovers.

The sauce is an amped up béchamel (milk sauce thickened with flour and butter) with some cheese for good measure. The crisped garlic on top is optional, but it adds a welcome little crunch to your bites.

2 tablespoons olive oil

2 cloves garlic, minced

¼ cup finely chopped onion

10 ounces baby spinach, coarsely chopped

½ teaspoon kosher salt

CREAM SAUCE

1 tablespoon butter

1 tablespoon flour

1¼ cups milk

2 tablespoons cream cheese

3 tablespoons finely grated Parmesan

Pinch nutmeg

1. In a medium nonstick skillet, heat olive oil, garlic and onion over medium heat. Sauté until onion is soft and just turning golden, 2 to 3 minutes.
2. Add spinach and salt and cook, stirring with tongs, until wilted. (Spinach can be added in batches, if needed, until all spinach has been cooked.) Transfer to a colander in the sink to drain.
3. For cream sauce: In the same skillet, melt butter over medium heat. Add flour and stir.
4. Whisk in milk, cream cheese, and Parmesan cheese. Stir until cream cheese is melted and sauce begins to thicken. Add nutmeg and remove from heat.
5. Press spinach in colander to release excess water, then add spinach to sauce. Stir until spinach is completely coated. Season to taste with salt.

TARA'S TIP

If you'd like crisped garlic chips for garnish, sauté sliced garlic in olive oil until golden, 1 to 2 minutes. Remove from oil and let cool to crisp.

SERVES

6 TO 8

HANDS-ON TIME

25 MINUTES

TOTAL TIME

1 HOUR 5 MINUTES

sheet pan potatoes

SOME ARE CRISPY and some are soft, but all of these thinly sliced potatoes are flavorful and tasty. This fun and different potato side dish cooks in the oven so you have your hands for other things.

The mandoline is a must for this recipe in order to make all the slices the same thickness, and it makes short work of the onion too. Wear a protective glove when slicing.

1½ pounds (3 medium) Yukon gold potatoes	¾ teaspoon kosher salt
	¼ teaspoon ground black pepper
¼ of a medium onion	2 tablespoons chopped parsley for garnish
3 tablespoons olive oil	

1. Heat oven to 375°F. Peel potatoes. Using a mandoline adjusted to a very thin setting, slice potatoes. Slices should be thin enough to bend but not thin enough to be transparent.
2. In a large bowl, cover potato slices with cold water and drain. Repeat twice then spread slices out on a clean towel or paper towels and pat dry.
3. Slice onion on the mandoline with the same setting. Roughly chop the slices and combine with rinsed and dried potatoes. Toss potatoes and onion with olive oil, salt, and pepper, coating evenly.
4. Arrange mixture on a parchment-lined rimmed baking sheet so potatoes are overlapping a bit. Bake until potatoes are tender, 35 to 40 minutes. You can use a spatula or tongs to move the potatoes around a bit as they cook so the edges don't get too brown and crispy. Serve warm, garnished with chopped parsley.

TARA'S TIP

If you don't have a mandoline, you can dice the potatoes instead. Just follow the recipe, cooking until the diced potatoes are tender.

waldorf salad with radicchio and buttermilk dressing

REALLY, THE RESEMBLANCE to classic Waldorf salad is just the combo of apples, celery, and grapes—but I just love that one of my favorite salads heralded from New York City, where I live. I'm paying a little homage to its history! With shaved apple, flavorful radicchio, and a light, savory buttermilk dressing, this updated version of Waldorf salad is elegant and welcoming. I made a tangy buttermilk herb dressing and opted for delicious candied pecans instead of walnuts.

I absolutely loved Waldorf salad when I was little, and here's why: instead of the classic mayo dressing, my mom covered the entire salad in sweetened whipped cream. I could eat the entire bowl, and who wouldn't with that kind of dressing?

SERVES

6 TO 8

MAKES

¾ CUPS DRESSING

HANDS-ON TIME

25 MINUTES

TOTAL TIME

30 MINUTES

TARA'S TIP

Radicchio is a very strong, sometimes bitter leafy vegetable. I think it's fantastic with tangy buttermilk and yogurt. But if you want a milder salad, opt for butter lettuce leaves.

CANDIED PECANS

3 tablespoons pure maple syrup

Pinch cayenne pepper

¾ cup (3 ounces) pecans

BUTTERMILK DRESSING

½ cup buttermilk

¼ cup plain Greek yogurt

1 tablespoon fresh lemon juice

1 tablespoon chopped chives

1 tablespoon chopped parsley, plus more for garnish

¼ teaspoon kosher salt

Pinch black pepper

SALAD

1 small head or half a large head radicchio (10 ounces)

1 apple, cored and cut in half

3 ribs celery, sliced on the bias

1½ cups California red grapes, sliced in half

1. For the pecans: Line a baking sheet with parchment and set aside. In a small skillet over medium heat, bring maple syrup and cayenne to a boil. Boil 1 minute, and then add pecans. Stir to coat and cook another 30 seconds. Turn onto lined baking sheet and separate nuts. Set aside and let cool completely. When cool, coarsely chop.

2. For the dressing: Whisk together all ingredients and set aside in the refrigerator.

3. For the salad: Break or chop radicchio into pieces. Use a mandoline or slicer to thinly slice apple. Arrange radicchio, apple, celery, and grapes in a bowl, then top with chopped pecans. You can toss with the dressing and extra parsley at this point, or you can serve the salad with the dressing and parsley on the side so guests can dress their own salad.

MAKES

1 LOAF

HANDS-ON TIME

20 MINUTES

TOTAL TIME

2 HOURS
30 MINUTES

dill bread

I GREW UP WITH my mom's dill-batter bread. It would make an appearance every once in a while on the dinner table, and I loved it, especially warm with loads of butter. I've modified the recipe to be a softer, loaf-style bread, but you can still bake it in a crock like Mom did. Or you can make rolls and bake them in a 9-inch square pan! However you enjoy this savory bread, you'll find it will become a family favorite very quickly.

1 package (2¼ teaspoons) instant yeast

¼ cup warm water

1 tablespoon granulated sugar

1 cup cottage cheese

1 scallion, minced

1 tablespoon dried dill (or 2 tablespoons chopped fresh dill)

½ teaspoon baking powder

1 teaspoon fine salt

2 large eggs, divided

2¼ cups (288 g) all-purpose flour

Maldon sea salt flakes

1. In the bowl of a stand mixer, whisk together the yeast, water, sugar, cottage cheese, scallion, dill, baking powder, salt, and 1 egg.

2. Fit the mixer with the dough hook. Add flour and mix to create a stiff dough. Let mixer knead dough on medium speed until a smooth and wet dough forms, scraping down sides of bowl as needed, about 4 minutes. Dough will pull away from the sides of the bowl in little sheets when ready.

3. Remove dough hook and scrape sides of bowl, forming dough into a ball. Spray dough and inside of bowl with cooking spray. Cover and set aside in a warm place to rise until almost doubled in size, about 1½ hours.

4. Grease an 8½-by-4½-inch loaf pan. Turn out dough onto a lightly floured surface and pat into an 8-by-10-inch rectangle, then roll into a tight log to shape into a standard loaf. Pinch seam to seal together and place in loaf pan, cover, and let rise until almost doubled in size, 30 to 40 minutes. While bread rises, heat oven to 350°F.

5. Beat remaining egg with a tablespoon of water to make an egg wash. Brush the top of the loaf with some egg wash and sprinkle with Maldon salt.

6. Bake loaf until top is golden brown and bread is cooked through, 25 to 30 minutes. Remove from oven and let cool in pan 5 minutes before turning out to cool completely.

green beans with shallot dressing

SERVES

8 TO 10

HANDS-ON TIME

25 MINUTES

TOTAL TIME

35 MINUTES

I CONSIDER THE simple green bean a canvas for any and all delicious flavors I want to add. They are so easy to prepare, so a few extra minutes for a tasty dressing, browned butter, or a candied nut are worth the effort.

To spruce them up to be worthy of a holiday meal, I've added a tangy dressing. The sharp vinegar quick-pickles the shallots for a unique topping. With ingredients you probably already have in the pantry, you can whip up this side dish anytime. Serve these beans with traditional turkey, roast chicken, pork tenderloin, pot roast (page 61), or braised short ribs.

¼ cup sherry vinegar

¼ teaspoon kosher salt

1 teaspoon sugar

3 tablespoons chopped shallot or red onion

6 tablespoons olive oil, divided

2 tablespoons chopped parsley

1 1-pound package thin green beans (haricot vert)

1. For the dressing: In a mixing bowl, whisk together sherry vinegar, salt, sugar, and shallot until sugar dissolves. Add 4 tablespoons oil and whisk to combine. Add parsley and set aside.

2. For the green beans: Heat remaining 2 tablespoons olive oil in a large skillet over medium-high heat. Add green beans and 2 tablespoons water and cook, stirring occasionally, until beans are tender-crisp, 7 to 8 minutes. Remove from heat.

3. Serve tossed or drizzled with some of the dressing.

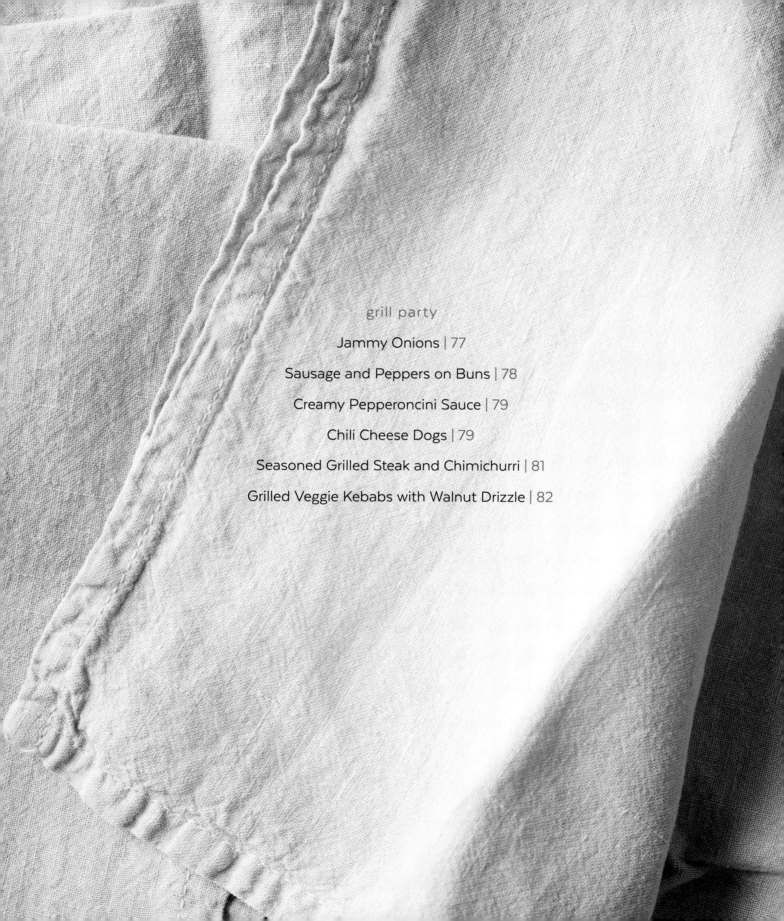

grill party

Don't resort to your standard burger menu when you gather friends together for a cookout. Try a few new recipes and see how that backyard party turns epic. I've solved any menu planning problems and given you all the recipes you need to make a great event.

There is something for everyone here, and it's all so good, everyone might eat all the somethings! There's steak and chimichurri, dogs and brats with amazing toppings, and veggie kebabs that even the meat eaters will dig. These all go well with some store-bought chips and plenty of ice-cold drinks.

jammy onions

SLOWLY COOKING ONIONS brings out their natural sugars and makes them sweet. I added some savory flavors to my caramelized onions to make a tangy, sweet, irresistible topping for my brats and sausages. Just use pantry staples like apple cider vinegar and spices!

Turns out these soft jam-like onions are also delicious on any sandwich, as a condiment on charcuterie boards, or spooned over mashed potatoes! I suggest keeping a jar in your fridge at all times.

MAKES

ABOUT 2 CUPS

HANDS-ON TIME

15 MINUTES

TOTAL TIME

40 MINUTES

3 tablespoons olive oil

4 medium yellow onions, sliced (6 cups sliced)

½ teaspoon kosher salt

2 bay leaves

⅓ cup apple cider vinegar

2 tablespoons light brown sugar

¼ teaspoon garlic powder

¼ teaspoon celery seeds

¼ teaspoon coriander

TARA'S TIP

Serve these onions with grilled brats or hot dogs. They are delicious paired with Creamy Pepperoncini Sauce (page 79) on any flavor brat.

1. Heat oil in a large nonstick skillet or Dutch oven over medium heat. Add onions, salt, and bay leaves. Use tongs to turn onions, coating them with oil. Cover and let cook for 10 minutes to soften, stirring every 3 to 4 minutes.

2. Add vinegar, brown sugar, and spices. Toss to coat evenly. Reduce heat to medium-low and cook, covered, another 10 minutes.

3. Uncover, stir, and cook until onions are very soft and liquid is gone, another 10 to 12 minutes. Stir frequently and reduce heat to low if needed so the onions don't overbrown.

4. Serve warm or at room temperature. Onions will keep airtight in the fridge for up to 2 weeks.

sausage and peppers on buns

A BOWL OF MELTY bell peppers is a classic go-to for grilled Italian sausages and a welcome condiment on any backyard BBQ table. I've left out the standard onions so you can add my Jammy Onions (page 77) to your bun with the peppers.

Make the peppers ahead of time and store them in the fridge, then zap them in the microwave or reheat them on the stove. Let everyone know they go on more than just their buns! They are tasty on top of steak, burgers, chicken, hot dogs, and grilled bread.

Pictured on page 72.

3 bell peppers (various colors)	6 sweet Italian sausages
2 tablespoons olive oil	6 hot dog buns or Italian rolls
½ teaspoon kosher salt	Creamy Pepperoncini Sauce (page 79)
1 tablespoon balsamic vinegar	Other condiments as desired

1. Seed and slice peppers into ¼-inch strips.
2. Heat oil in a large skillet over medium-high heat. Add peppers and salt. Stir to coat with oil and reduce heat to medium. Cook, stirring occasionally, until peppers are just soft and charred in parts, 6 to 8 minutes.
3. Add balsamic vinegar and stir to coat, then remove from heat and set aside.
4. Heat a gas or charcoal grill to medium heat. Roll Italian sausages on a clean work suface to make them a bit thinner and longer because they will shrink on the grill. Grill sausages on a covered grill 8 to 10 minutes, turning occasionally.
5. Spread buns with pepperoncini sauce and other condiments if desired, and add sausages and some peppers. You can also let everyone build their own.
6. Cooked peppers will keep airtight in the fridge for up to a week.

creamy pepperoncini sauce

THIS CREAMY SAUCE is made with ingredients you may already have on hand. You'll love it as a condiment at the BBQ, but it's also tasty with crackers, pita chips, or potato chips. The flavors meld and combine if you make this ahead!

Pictured on page 76 with the JAMMY ONIONS.

Pictured on page 76 with the JAMMY ONIONS.

½ cup plain Greek yogurt

2 tablespoons mayonnaise

⅓ cup finely chopped pepperoncini

¼ teaspoon red pepper flakes

Kosher salt

Stir together yogurt, mayonnaise, pepperoncini, and red pepper flakes. Season to taste with salt. This sauce can be stored in the refrigerator for up to 5 days.

MAKES

¾ CUP

TOTAL TIME

10 MINUTES

chili cheese dogs

MY HOMEMADE Pepper Jack Nacho Cheese (page 103) and Blue-Ribbon Beef-and-Bacon Chili (page 137) show off here on top of a humble hot dog. This hot dog is an ode to the Nathan's chili cheese dog I must have with every visit to Coney Island! I love them more than I should. Minus the roller coasters, you'll feel like you're walking the boardwalk with cheesy goodness dripping from your chin.

Both toppings can be made ahead of time, so these dogs are great for a weekend party or weeknight dinner with the kids.

Pictured on page 73.

Pictured on page 73.

8 hot dog buns

8 hot dogs

Half a recipe Blue-Ribbon Beef-and-Bacon Chili (page 137)

Half a recipe Pepper Jack Nacho Cheese (page 103)

Pickled jalapeños (optional)

1. Heat gas or charcoal grill to medium-high. Grill hot dogs until heated through, 5 to 7 minutes.
2. Meanwhile, heat chili and nacho cheese.
3. To assemble, add hot dogs to buns, then top with chili, cheese sauce, and pickled jalapeños if you'd like.

SERVES

8

TOTAL TIME

15 MINUTES, NOT INCLUDING RECIPE PREP

TARA'S TIP

If serving these on a make-your-own buffet, you can keep the nacho cheese warm in a slow cooker on low heat. Stir occasionally to keep smooth.

GATHER-AROUND DINNERS

seasoned grilled steak and chimichurri

LIKE PB&J. A wink and a smile. Cookies and milk. What I'm trying to say here is that herby, tangy chimichurri and grilled steak are the perfect pair! They are a genius combination, and don't forget the toasty bread! Grilled, crispy bread slathered with extra chimichurri is divine.

The cumin and salt do wonders for the steak. I think you'll make this your go-to steak seasoning from now on. You truly need no sauce or extra spice; it's perfectly balanced.

So try this pair on for size. I imagine this meal will be your peas and carrots, your Romeo and Juliet, and your moon and stars like it is mine!

MAKES

¾ CUP CHIMICHURRI

SERVES

4 TO 6

HANDS-ON TIME

30 MINUTES

TOTAL TIME

1 HOUR 10 MINUTES

CHIMICHURRI

- 2 cloves garlic, minced
- ½ cup finely chopped flat-leaf parsley
- ⅓ cup extra-virgin olive oil
- 3 tablespoons finely chopped shallot or red onion
- 2 tablespoons chopped oregano
- 2 tablespoons finely chopped cilantro
- 2 tablespoons sherry vinegar or red wine vinegar
- 2 tablespoons fresh lemon juice
- 2 tablespoons honey
- 1 teaspoon kosher salt
- ½ teaspoon ground cumin
- ⅛ teaspoon cayenne pepper

GRILLED STEAK

- 4 New York strip or rib-eye steaks
- 1 tablespoon ground cumin
- 1 tablespoon kosher salt
- 1 loaf ciabatta or rustic French bread
- Extra-virgin olive oil for brushing
- Olive oil

1. For the chimichurri: In a bowl, combine all chimichurri ingredients. Set aside. Stir occasionally until ready to serve.
2. For the steak: Pat steaks dry with a paper towel, then rub them all over with a mixture of the cumin and salt. Set aside to rest for 20 to 30 minutes at room temperature.
3. Heat grill to medium heat. Slice bread into thick slices and brush with olive oil. Set aside.
4. Grill steaks to medium doneness (145°F using a meat thermometer), 5 to 7 minutes on each side. Let steak rest about 5 minutes before serving.
5. Grill bread until just charred and crisped
6. Serve steak and bread with chimichurri.

SERVES

6 TO 8

MAKES

8 KEBABS

TOTAL TIME

45 MINUTES

grilled veggie kebabs with walnut drizzle

SIMPLE GRILLED VEGETABLES become extraordinary with a spoonful of my walnut dressing and are a great option for those vegetarians or veggie lovers at your BBQ party. Thread any variety of tender vegetables on skewers and give them a smoky char on the grill. Your vegetables should be cut to about the same size so they cook at the same rate; 1-to-1½-inch pieces will be perfect.

TARA'S TIP

Bamboo skewers will burn on a grill if they aren't soaked first. In a shallow baking dish, cover the skewers with water and let sit for 30 minutes before using them for kebabs.

WALNUT LEMON DRESSING

½ large shallot, minced

½ cup finely chopped walnuts

3 tablespoons fresh lemon juice

2 tablespoons water

1 tablespoon honey

1 teaspoon Dijon mustard

½ teaspoon lemon zest

½ teaspoon kosher salt

Pinch red pepper flakes

¼ cup extra-virgin olive oil

VEGETABLE KEBABS

6 cups (about 1½ pounds) tender vegetables cut into pieces (such as zucchini, summer squash, baby bell peppers, cherry tomatoes, button mushrooms, and asparagus)

8 metal skewers or soaked bamboo skewers

Olive oil for brushing

Kosher salt

1. For the dressing: In a medium bowl, whisk together everything except olive oil. Then whisk in olive oil and set aside. Stir again before serving.
2. For the kebabs: Heat grill to medium. Divide vegetables between skewers, threading them on in various orders. Brush kebabs with olive oil and sprinkle lightly with salt.
3. Grill kebabs, turning occasionally, until vegetables are charred in places and just tender-crisp, about 10 minutes.
4. Drizzle kebabs with dressing and serve with extra dressing on the side.

SERIOUS SIDES

We all love an accessory, a trimming, or a really great complement! That's just what this chapter is all about. While I could make a meal from a few of these delicious side dishes, they are meant to be eaten alongside something of main-dish status. They complement and accessorize even the simplest of meals. You will see that I'm serious about my sides, and I know you'll find them seriously delicious.

There are salads, breads (like my soft and sweet cornbread), dips, veggies, and more on the following pages. Try the herby mac and cheese for a heavenly experience, or go for the simple buttery rice pilaf when you need a side dish that doesn't take center stage.

These sides are meant to be eaten with many of the recipes in this book, but feel free to mix and match them to your own menus and favorite meals. The party dips and tarte soleil may become traditions for your gatherings, and the baked beans will be a go-to for any BBQ or game-day event.

bbq baked beans

I ALWAYS TRY THE BEANS at BBQ restaurants I visit, and every one has a different recipe. That's a good thing! The sides to your signature BBQ should be made with as much care as that brisket or those ribs.

I've created my own here, and just like a signature pitmaster's sauce, it's loaded with a combination of seasonings to hit your taste buds just right. These beans go perfectly with my Texas-Style Beef Brisket (page 155) or my Spicy Honey-Lime Chicken (page 162). Get creative: add more heat, throw in more sugar, use smoked paprika, or add your own secret ingredient. Then spoon leftovers on a baked potato for dinner the next day!

SERVES

8 TO 10

MAKES

7 CUPS

HANDS-ON TIME

25 MINUTES

TOTAL TIME

1 HOUR 45 MINUTES

8 ounces bacon (about 7 slices), cut into ½-inch pieces

1 medium onion, finely chopped

1 green bell pepper, finely diced

1 small jalapeño, finely chopped

5 cloves garlic, minced

3 (15-ounce) cans pinto beans, drained

1 to 2 tablespoons dark brown sugar

1 tablespoon Worcestershire sauce

1 tablespoon prepared yellow mustard

¼ cup apple cider vinegar

½ cup molasses (not blackstrap)

½ cup ketchup

½ cup canned crushed tomatoes

½ cup BBQ sauce

1 tablespoon paprika

½ teaspoon garlic powder

½ teaspoon onion powder

¼ teaspoon cayenne pepper

1 teaspoon kosher salt

¼ teaspoon red pepper flakes

1 cup water

1. Heat oven to 325°F with rack in the center of the oven. Heat a 6-quart Dutch oven with a tight-fitting lid over medium-low heat. Add the bacon and cook, stirring occasionally, until fat is rendered and bacon is just crispy, about 10 minutes. Use a slotted spoon to transfer bacon to a bowl; set aside. Add onions, peppers, and garlic to the pot with the rendered bacon fat and cook until onions are soft, stirring occasionally, 4 to 5 minutes.

2. Add the cooked bacon back to the pot with the beans and all seasonings and sauces. Add 1 cup water and stir to combine. Cover the pot and transfer to the oven. Bake, covered, in the oven until flavors have combined and sauce has thickened, 45 minutes to 1 hour. Stir beans once during cooking time.

3. Remove from oven and let stand for 5 to 10 minutes before serving. Cooled leftovers can be stored in the refrigerator for up to a week.

TARA'S TIP

The amount of brown sugar you use will depend on the sweetness of your BBQ sauce. If your sauce is sweet, use only 1 tablespoon brown sugar. If it's on the savory or spicy side, use 2 tablespoons.

Bake the beans for 45 minutes if you prefer them saucier and for 1 hour for thicker, heartier beans.

SERVES

9

MAKES

1 (8-INCH)
SQUARE PAN

HANDS-ON TIME

15 MINUTES

TOTAL TIME

55 MINUTES

TARA'S TIP

To double the recipe,
prepare a 9-by-13-
inch baking dish
or pan. Double all
the ingredients and
bake an additional
10 to 15 minutes.

Make this cornbread
gluten-free by
swapping the
all-purpose flour for
GF all-purpose flour.
I recommend the
Cup4Cup brand
for an identical
texture and taste.
Gluten-free cornbread
takes 10 to 15 minutes
longer to cook.

golden sweet cornbread

THIS DELIGHTFULLY FLUFFY, perfectly sweetened cornbread goes with anything and is excellent on its own. If there are ever leftovers, they end up as my breakfast the next day!

There are definitely two camps when it comes to cornbread: the sweet, cakey fans and the more savory, traditional fans. I love any cornbread but am really partial to this soft, cake-like version. The texture is tender and pleasant, and the corn flavor still gets through with a hint of honey.

Serve this with butter or cinnamon honey butter, and you can add corn kernels too. It is a great side to my Texas-Style Beef Brisket (page 155), Blue-Ribbon Beef-and-Bacon Chili (page 137), chicken dinner, and soups. I even use it as a shortcake base for my Blackberry and Peach Cornbread Shortcake (page 210)—it's that amazing!

½ cup yellow cornmeal	3 tablespoons butter, melted
1½ cups all-purpose flour	⅓ cup canola or avocado oil
⅔ cup granulated sugar	2 large eggs
½ teaspoon fine salt	1 tablespoon honey
1 tablespoon baking powder	1¼ cups whole milk

1. Heat oven to 350°F. Grease an 8-by-8-inch square pan or a 1½-to-2-quart baking dish. Set aside.
2. In a medium mixing bowl, combine cornmeal, flour, sugar, salt, and baking powder. Whisk together and set aside.
3. In another bowl or large measuring cup, combine melted butter, oil, eggs, honey, and milk. Whisk until eggs are broken up and blended.
4. Pour milk mixture into dry ingredients. Whisk until smooth and just combined.
5. Transfer batter to prepared baking dish and smooth into an even layer with a spatula. Bake 30 to 35 minutes or until a toothpick inserted in the center comes out almost clean (with no wet batter).
6. Cool for a few minutes and serve warm, or cool completely.

grape and feta quinoa

THIS IS MY FAVORITE grain salad with all the crunchy nuts, salty feta, herbs, and juicy grapes. The light, tangy dressing is just enough to season the salad, and you can serve this quinoa with just about anything. Try it with pork chops, roast chicken, or the Red Pepper and Burrata Burgers (page 146). It's good in the summer, at a picnic, with your weeknight meal, or with Thanksgiving dinner. Delicious California grapes come in green, red, or black, and you can use any color you like.

1 cup quinoa

2 cups water

Pinch salt

1 cup (6 ounces) California grapes, halved

⅔ cup (3 ounces) crumbled feta

⅓ cup (1 ounce) walnuts, toasted and broken up

⅓ cup chopped flat-leaf parsley

DRESSING

Grated zest from 1 lemon

3 tablespoons fresh lemon juice

1 small clove garlic, minced

¼ teaspoon kosher salt

2 tablespoons olive oil

1. To cook quinoa, rinse in a fine mesh strainer until the water runs clear. Transfer to a medium saucepan with water and salt. Bring to a boil, then lower heat and simmer, uncovered, until quinoa is tender and liquid is absorbed, about 15 minutes. Remove from heat and cool.
2. While quinoa cooks, make dressing by whisking together all dressing ingredients. Set aside.
3. When quinoa is cool, add grapes, feta, walnuts, and parsley. Toss with dressing and serve. Quinoa can be refrigerated for up to a day.

SERVES

6 TO 8

MAKES

4 CUPS

HANDS-ON TIME

15 MINUTES

TOTAL TIME

30 MINUTES

SERIOUS SIDES

roast carrots with lemon feta dip

THESE OVEN-BAKED CARROTS are extra delicious when paired with a tangy, creamy feta dip. Serve the carrots as a side dish to a chicken dinner, pot roast, or fish, or cut them into small sticks and serve with the dip as a snack or appetizer. The bits of crunchy crumbs add a fun texture.

You'll find the garlicky lemon feta dip great for dipping any veggies, cooked or raw, as well as a great spread for pita and crackers. Get creative with it—it's your new favorite dip!

CRUMBS

½ cup Panko breadcrumbs

2 tablespoons finely grated Parmesan

1 tablespoon butter, melted

2 teaspoons chopped fresh oregano

CARROTS

15 slender carrots, peeled and trimmed

1 clove garlic, minced

½ teaspoon kosher salt

½ teaspoon Aleppo pepper

1 teaspoon chopped fresh oregano

1 teaspoon honey

1½ tablespoons olive oil

FETA DIP

½ cup (4 ounces) crumbled feta cheese

1 cup (8 ounces) plain Greek yogurt

1 teaspoon lemon zest

2 teaspoons fresh lemon juice

1 clove garlic, minced

1 teaspoon chopped fresh oregano (or ½ teaspoon dried)

½ teaspoon Aleppo pepper, plus extra for sprinkling

1. Heat oven to 375°F. Add the Panko to a medium mixing bowl, and stir in the parmesan and melted butter. Spread out on a baking sheet and toast in the oven just until lightly golden, about 7 minutes. Let cool, then stir in chopped oregano; set aside.

2. Cut large carrots in half lengthwise and leave others whole. (Alternatively cut carrots into ½-inch sticks). On a rimmed baking sheet, toss the carrots with the garlic, salt, Aleppo pepper, oregano, honey, and olive oil.

3. Bake until carrots are tender-crisp and caramelized in parts, turning with a spatula halfway through, 25 to 30 minutes.

4. While the carrots cook, make the feta dip: In the bowl of an electric mixer fitted with the paddle attachment, or with a hand mixer, blend together the feta, yogurt, lemon zest and juice, garlic, oregano and pepper. Mix until almost smooth. Transfer to a serving bowl and sprinkle with extra Aleppo pepper.

5. Serve carrots hot from the oven alongside the dip.

TARA'S TIP

Double this recipe to feed a crowd. The carrots will fit on two baking sheets; rotate them in the oven halfway through cooking.

The feta dip can be made in advance and stored in the fridge up to a week.

Aleppo pepper comes from the Halaby pepper, a dark-burgundy-colored chili that is dried and crushed to create the spice. It has a mild heat with hints of cumin and sundried tomatoes and gives dishes a glorious bit of heat and flavor.

spinach and artichoke tarte soleil

THIS SAVORY TART is a showstopper on the table and yet is incredibly easy to make. My friend Laura showed me how to make this design, and now I'm hooked! The design works for all kinds of fillings.

This particular filling takes a note from one of my favorite dips. I nestle my own veggie, herb, and cheese mixture between two sheets of flaky puff pastry, then twist it into its eye-catching pattern. This pull-apart, sharable dish is ideal as an appetizer, with soup or salad, or alongside your favorite main dish.

SERVES

8 TO 10

MAKES

1 TART

HANDS-ON TIME

35 MINUTES

TOTAL TIME

1 HOUR 15 MINUTES

TARTE SOLEIL

- ½ cup (2 ounces) crumbled feta cheese
- 2 cups packed (3½ ounces) spinach leaves
- ¼ cup chopped scallions
- Half a can (14-ounce) artichoke hearts, drained and rinsed

- 2 tablespoons chopped fresh dill (or 1 teaspoon dried)
- 1 large egg
- 1 tablespoon water
- All-purpose flour for dusting
- 1 (17.5-ounce) box puff pastry, thawed
- Sesame seeds

DILL TOPPING

- 1 tablespoon finely chopped flat-leaf parsley
- 1 tablespoon chopped fresh dill

- 2 tablespoons chopped scallions
- Zest from half a lemon
- 1 tablespoon honey

> **TARA'S TIP**
>
> This tart can be made up to 6 hours in advance. Keep loosely covered at room temperature until ready to serve.
>
> Puff pastry can be found in your grocery freezer section and shouldn't be confused for phyllo dough.

1. For the tart: Heat oven to 375°F with rack in lower third. Line a baking sheet with parchment. Set aside.

2. To the bowl of a food processor fitted with the blade attachment, add feta, spinach, scallions, artichokes, and dill. Pulse until very finely chopped, almost smooth.

3. In a small bowl, whisk egg and water to make an egg wash. Set aside.

4. On a lightly floured surface, use a rolling pin to roll one of the sheets of puff pastry into a 12-by-12-inch square. Cut a 12-inch-diameter circle out of the puff pastry using a plate or mixing bowl as a guide. Place the round on the parchment-lined baking sheet. Repeat with the second sheet of puff pastry. Discard dough scraps.

5. Spread the feta cheese mixture evenly over the round of puff pastry on the baking sheet, leaving a ½-inch border around the edge.

6. Brush some of the egg wash around the edge of the puff pastry. Place the second round of puff pastry on top, gently pressing the edges of the circle to seal.

7. Using the rim of a 3-inch-diameter cup or bowl, press gently in the center of the puff pastry to make an indentation without pressing all the way through the pastry dough. This indentation will guide your cutting. Use a knife to cut strips

Continued on next page

from the indentation to the outside edge of the circle. (Leave the strips attached to the inner circle, like sunbeams coming out of a sun.) Cut the circle into quarters, then cut each quarter in half to create eighths. Cut each eighth into three pieces to make twenty-four strips total. Then carefully twist each strip of puff pastry twice without breaking the pieces off.

8. Brush entire tart with remaining egg wash. Sprinkle with a few teaspoons of sesame seeds.

9. Bake 30 to 35 minutes, until pastry is golden brown. Let cool before serving.

10. For topping: Combine parsley, dill, scallions, and lemon zest. When tart is ready to serve, drizzle with honey and sprinkle with herb mixture.

1. Roll out sheets of puff pastry and cut into two 12-inch-diameter circles. Spread one with filling, leaving a ½-inch border.
2. Egg wash the edge and top with second circle.
3. Use a glass to indent the center for a guide. Cut strips from the indentation to the outside edge of the circle, making twenty-four equal strips.
4. Twist each strip twice to make design. Egg wash the top before baking.

asparagus and peas with parmesan breadcrumbs

SERVES

6 TO 8

HANDS-ON TIME

25 MINUTES

TOTAL TIME

40 MINUTES

TO ME THIS is the ultimate vegetable side dish—bright green, flavorful, and beautiful. Since asparagus is available almost all year, you can serve it with all sorts of meals: for a Sunday dinner, on Mother's Day, at Easter, or on Thanksgiving. The toasty breadcrumbs can be made days in advance and are tasty on top of any veggie.

BREADCRUMBS

2 slices day-or-two-old sourdough or French bread

Zest of 1 lemon

¼ cup grated Parmesan

1 tablespoon olive oil

ASPARAGUS

1 (1-pound) bunch asparagus

2 tablespoons olive oil

½ teaspoon kosher salt

1 cup fresh or frozen peas

3 scallions, white and green parts chopped

1 tablespoon fresh lemon juice

2 teaspoons chopped fresh mint, plus more for garnish

⅓ cup crushed pistachios

TARA'S TIP

Depending on the herbs you find or have on hand, or your family preferences, you can substitute basil, dill, or parsley for the mint.

1. For the breadcrumbs: Heat oven to 350°F. Line a small baking sheet with parchment.

2. Tear bread into pieces. Blend bread pieces in a food processor with lemon zest and cheese until bread turns into coarse crumbs. Add olive oil and pulse to combine well.

3. Spread bread crumbs evenly on prepared baking sheet. Bake until light brown and crisped, 12 to 14 minutes. You may want to stir them once to ensure even browning. Let cool completely before using. Crumbs can be stored in an airtight container for up to 3 days.

4. For the asparagus: Trim woody ends off asparagus. Slice on the bias into 1-to-1½-inch pieces.

5. Heat oil in a large nonstick skillet over medium-high heat. Add asparagus and salt. Cook, stirring, until asparagus starts to get bright green, about 2 minutes. Add peas, scallions, and lemon juice and cook until asparagus is just tender, 2 minutes more.

6. Remove from heat and add mint and pistachios. Serve topped with breadcrumbs and garnished with extra mint if desired.

SERVES

12 TO 14

MAKES ABOUT

7 CUPS

TOTAL TIME

40 MINUTES

TARA'S TIP

In order to create this look, you need enough dip ingredients for a large crowd. For smaller groups, halve the recipe. "Load" your dip however you wish on your platter or layer it in a glass dish.

It's tricky to get perfect rings of toppings on your first try. You can start in the middle with the corn and work outward if that is easier for you!

loaded guacamole dip

TURN THAT FAMOUS seven-layer dip on its head! You know the one; I've got a gorgeous version on my blog. Here, I've loaded a tasty layer of guacamole with so much good stuff (and some new additions). I wanted a dip that could serve as a centerpiece, so I've composed the platter to look impressive. It's a showstopper that's perfect for dipping your chips into, scooping onto enchiladas, or dolloping on a taco salad. Your taste buds will know what to expect—amazingness!

I suggest making your own simple guacamole with my quick-cheat tomatillo salsa recipe provided here. But in a pinch, you can buy the guac. I won't tell.

TACO CREMA

1¼ cups sour cream	3 tablespoons taco seasoning

GUACAMOLE

5 ripe avocados	⅓ cup chopped cilantro
1 teaspoon kosher salt	2 tablespoons fresh lime juice
½ cup green tomatillo salsa	

GREEN SALSA

¾ cup chopped cilantro	2 tablespoons finely diced jalapeño
⅓ cup finely chopped scallions	

TOPPINGS

1¼ to 1½ cups finely diced tomatoes, seeds removed and drained of juice	Half a can (15-ounce) black beans, drained and rinsed
1 to 1¼ cups crumbled cotija cheese	¾ cup roasted corn kernels
	Chips for serving

1. For the taco crema: In a medium bowl, whisk together sour cream and taco seasoning. Set aside in the fridge while you prepare the remaining elements.

2. For the guacamole: In a large bowl, smash all guacamole ingredients until you achieve a slightly chunky consistency. Cover and set aside.

3. For the green salsa: Mix together all green salsa ingredients. Set aside.

4. Prepare remaining toppings.

5. On a large platter (I used an oval platter 12-by-14- or 12-by-16-inches), spread guacamole in a ¼- to ½-inch-thick layer. Gently spread taco crema on guacamole in a single layer, leaving a border of guacamole. Carefully create a ring of chopped tomatoes near the edge of the sour cream, then do the same with a smaller ring of cotija cheese. Continue making rings with the green salsa and the black beans, finishing with the corn in the center. Make sure to create very skinny rings so there is room for each ingredient.

6. Serve immediately with chips, or cover and refrigerate for up to an hour.

pepper jack nacho cheese

MY QUESO IS MELTY HEAVEN in a bowl. And there's no need to chop your own peppers because I use Pepper Jack cheese for a kick of flavor! Sharp cheddar and spices from your cupboard are the other additions that make this dip a crowd-pleaser.

In my first book, *Live Life Deliciously,* I told you about sodium citrate: the natural substance that prevents cheese from curdling or separating and makes a cheese sauce ultra-smooth and reheatable. It's my secret ingredient and is a must for a really dreamy nacho cheese. You can order food-grade sodium citrate online.

Use this sauce for the Chili Cheese Dogs (page 79), the Chili Cheese Fries (page 104), and Ultimate Chili con Queso (page 107).

1½ cups whipping cream

½ teaspoon sodium citrate

¼ teaspoon onion powder

¼ teaspoon garlic powder

⅛ teaspoon ground cumin

2 cups (8 ounces) shredded sharp cheddar cheese

2 cups (8 ounces) shredded Pepper Jack cheese

TOPPINGS

Jalapeños

Diced red bell pepper

Tomatoes

Scallions

1. In a saucepan over medium-high heat, cook cream until warm and bubbling around the edges. Reduce heat.
2. Stir in sodium citrate and seasonings.
3. Add cheese in batches, a cup or two at a time. Stir, allowing cheese to melt between batches. Do not boil.
4. Serve warm, topped with desired toppings. Store in the fridge for up to a week. To reheat, add a bit of milk or cream to thin the cheese, and gently heat on the stove or in the microwave, stirring frequently.

TARA'S TIP

Stir a desired amount of this nacho cheese over cooked pasta, top it with finely crumbled tortilla chips and the fresh toppings, and serve it as a mac and cheese. You'll love it!

SERVES

6 TO 8

HANDS-ON TIME

20 MINUTES

TOTAL TIME

30 MINUTES,
NOT INCLUDING
CHEESE AND
CHILI PREP

chili cheese fries

WHETHER IT'S GAME DAY, the weekend, or just a Tuesday, these loaded potatoes are the ultimate crowd-pleaser. These fries are the perfect way to use leftover Blue-Ribbon Beef-and-Bacon Chili (page 137) and Pepper Jack Nacho Cheese (page 103)—or they're the perfect excuse to make them!

The potato wedges are seasoned so they are actually delicious on their own, but adding melty cheese, meaty chili, and fresh toppings will make all your troubles disappear, if just for a moment of bliss.

TARA'S TIP

Store-bought salsa or pico de gallo is great as a topping. If you want to make your own, stir together some chopped white onion, diced tomato, cilantro, jalapeño, a splash of lime juice, and a sprinkle of salt.

POTATOES

4 small russet potatoes, scrubbed

3 tablespoons canola or avocado oil

½ teaspoon smoked paprika

½ teaspoon chili powder

½ teaspoon garlic powder

¼ teaspoon kosher salt

TOPPINGS

1½ cups Blue-Ribbon Beef-and-Bacon Chili (page 137)

1½ cups Pepper Jack Nacho Cheese (page 103)

Chopped cilantro

Pico de gallo (store-bought or homemade)

Avocados (optional)

1. Heat oven to 400°F. Slice potatoes in half lengthwise, then cut into 8 to 10 wedges each. In a large bowl, cover wedges with very cold water and let sit for 20 minutes. Then drain and pat dry with a paper towel.

2. Toss potatoes with oil and all seasonings, coating evenly. Spread wedges on a large rimmed baking sheet. Bake until golden and tender, 20 to 25 minutes.

3. On the baking sheet or a serving platter, gather half the potato wedges into a snug single layer. Spoon on some chili and nacho cheese sauce, then add the remaining potato wedges. Add the remaining chili and cheese and garnish with desired toppings. Serve immediately, or keep in a warm oven up to 30 minutes.

the ultimate chili con queso

THE NAME *CHILI CON QUESO* means "chili with cheese" and can be as simple as a melted cheese dip with hot chilis, or it can have beef or sausage chili stirred right in. You've perhaps had the version with Velveeta and canned chili, but I dare you to ever want that again after you try this dip. A mix of a spur-slinging chili and homemade nacho cheese sauce makes the best chili con queso you've ever tasted. Keep it warm in a slow cooker on your buffet table, or serve it to your guests in a cast-iron skillet. Either way, you'll all be huddled around finishing it off as fast as you can!

1½ cups Blue-Ribbon Beef-and-
Bacon Chili (page 137)

2 cups Pepper Jack Nacho Cheese
(page 103)

OPTIONAL TOPPINGS

Tomatoes

Fresh Green Salsa (page 52)

Jalapeños

Avocados

Chips

Sliced French bread (page 110)

1. In a medium saucepan or cast-iron skillet, heat chili until warm. Add nacho cheese and stir together.
2. Add toppings as desired and serve with chips or bread for dipping.

SERVES

8 TO 10

MAKES ABOUT

3½ CUPS

TOTAL TIME

15 MINUTES,
NOT INCLUDING
CHEESE AND
CHILI PREP

avocado salad

A SIMPLE SALAD of buttery, ripe avocados is often served on the side of Puerto Rican or South American meals. Sometimes it's served with crisp lettuce, other times with a spicy garlic sauce or pickled onions. I serve this with my Red Beans and Rice (page 128). Also try it with my Spicy Honey-Lime Chicken (page 162) or Seasoned Grilled Steak and Chimichurri (page 81).

SERVES

4 TO 6

HANDS-ON TIME

15 MINUTES

TOTAL TIME

35 MINUTES

2 tablespoons red wine vinegar

1½ tablespoons fresh lime juice

1 teaspoon granulated sugar

2 tablespoons avocado or olive oil

¼ of a small red onion, thinly sliced

2 ripe avocados, pitted and sliced

½ head iceberg lettuce, cut into wedges

Flaky sea salt and pepper

1. In a medium bowl, whisk together vinegar, lime juice, and sugar until sugar is dissolved. Whisk in oil, then add sliced red onion. Toss to coat and let sit for at least 20 minutes or up to a day in the fridge.
2. Arrange avocado slices and lettuce on a plate or platter. Drizzle with the pickled red onions and dressing. Sprinkle with salt and pepper to serve.

SERVES

10 TO 12

MAKES

2 LARGE LOAVES

HANDS-ON TIME

25 MINUTES

TOTAL TIME

2 HOURS
25 MINUTES

TARA'S TIP

Bread flour has
more protein than
all-purpose, so it
creates a different
texture in bread. I like
the mix here, and if
you're willing to keep
bread flour around,
it is worth it! In a
pinch, you can totally
make this bread with
only all-purpose
flour, using 6 cups
instead of 3 and 3.

easy french bread

THIS IS THE HOMEMADE French bread I grew up with. It often accompanied soup—usually mom's creamy chicken noodle—but it goes perfectly with anything. I've changed the original recipe just a bit, adjusting for flavor and texture. It's not the crusty rustic loaf you spend hours making; it's closer to the grocery store bakery loaves, with a supersoft, uniform texture.

Making this bread creates that luxurious scent of fresh bread in your house with hardly any hands-on time. The beauty of this recipe is that it stays in the mixer while it proofs, and the kneading happens just a little, every ten minutes. You can put your feet up or prep some soup while you wait.

YEAST

2 tablespoons active dry yeast	1 teaspoon granulated sugar
½ cup warm water	

BREAD

2 cups warm water	1¾ teaspoons fine salt
5 tablespoons olive oil	3 cups (384 g) bread flour
2 tablespoons granulated sugar	3 cups (384 g) all-purpose flour

1. Dissolve yeast in warm water with sugar. Let sit 5 minutes to bloom.
2. In the bowl of an electric mixer fitted with the dough hook, combine bloomed yeast with remaining bread ingredients. Mix well, about 2 minutes. Dough will be sticky.
3. Cover mixer with a lid, plastic wrap, or a thick towel. Let rest 10 minutes. Turn the mixer on and knead the dough for 10 to 20 seconds. Repeat this every 10 minutes, (for a total of 5 more kneads over 60 minutes).
4. Meanwhile, line a baking sheet with parchment. Set aside.
5. After you've kneaded the dough for the sixth time, prepare a lightly floured or oiled work surface. Punch down dough and divide into 2 equal parts. Roll each part into a rough 10-by-10-inch rectangle. Then roll each rectangle into a long loaf, pinching ends under.
6. Place loaves about 2 inches apart on baking sheet. Cover loosely with plastic wrap or a clean towel and let proof until almost doubled in size, about 30 minutes.
7. While bread proves, heat oven to 400°F.
8. Gently cut slits in the top of each loaf, then bake until golden brown and cooked through, 22 to 24 minutes. Let cool slightly and serve.

NOTE You can use instant yeast here instead of active dry. Just add the instant yeast, water, and teaspoon of sugar to the other ingredients in step 2. There's no need to bloom instant yeast.

buttery rice pilaf
with vermicelli

THIS DISH SHOULD BE a basic go-to in your arsenal. This flavorful yet simple rice side is a meal-planner's dream and goes with just about anything! If you're entertaining a crowd or just want a quick side even the kids will love, this recipe is your hero.

For classic pilaf, stick to American long-grain rice or even converted rice. Varieties like jasmine or basmati are too long for my taste, and the grains tend to break in a pilaf.

Find vermicelli in the pasta aisle. Toasting it in a dry pan gives it its brown color.

I like to serve this with Spicy Honey-Lime Chicken (page 162) or Blackened Salmon with Mango-Lime Salsa (page 158), and I add sliced almonds when I serve this with Skirt Steak with Strawberry Chimichurri (page 123).

SERVES

8 TO 10

MAKES

ABOUT 8 CUPS

HANDS-ON TIME

20 MINUTES

TOTAL TIME

40 MINUTES

½ cup uncooked vermicelli	2 cups long-grain white rice
5 tablespoons unsalted butter	1 teaspoon kosher salt
1 tablespoon avocado or canola oil	4 cups low-sodium chicken broth
1½ cups very finely diced onion	Minced parsley for garnish (optional)

1. Heat a 3½-to-4-quart saucepan over medium-high heat. Add dry vermicelli to hot pan and stir occasionally until toasted and golden brown, 2 to 3 minutes. Remove to a bowl and set aside.

2. Reduce heat to medium-low. Add butter, oil, and onion to pan. Cook, stirring occasionally, until onions are very soft and some are just turning golden, 6 to 7 minutes.

3. Increase heat to medium-high again and add the toasted vermicelli, rice, and salt to pan. Stir to coat rice with butter, then add chicken broth. Stir to combine.

4. Bring to a simmer. Once simmering, cover and reduce heat to medium-low or low to maintain simmer. Cook until almost all the liquid is absorbed and holes appear on the top of the rice, 13 to 14 minutes.

5. Turn off heat and leave covered for 15 to 20 minutes. Fluff with a fork and serve. Garnish with minced parsley if desired.

TARA'S TIP

If you can't find a bag of tiny vermicelli bits, find a box of vermicelli or angel hair pasta and crush the noodles in a zip-top bag with a rolling pin to create little pieces.

For a half batch, halve all ingredients, cook 12 to 13 minutes, then let rest, covered, 10 to 15 minutes.

SERVES

4 TO 6

HANDS-ON TIME

20 MINUTES

TOTAL TIME

55 MINUTES

cauliflower and couscous gratin

SOME OF MY FAVORITE RECIPES are iterations of things I developed years ago. This is one of them, and I've simplified it and made it more creamy and decadent. The cheesy cauliflower cooks on top of couscous, softening it and flavoring it all at once. Toasting the couscous creates a nutty taste that complements the richness of the cheese.

This dish perfectly accompanies roast chicken, BBQ, pork tenderloin or chops, and ribs or beef roast. The beauty of this dish is that it can actually be a pasta main dish along with a salad if you'd like.

1 cup Israeli (large-grain) couscous

2 pounds cauliflower florets (from 2 small whole cauliflowers)

2 cups (8 ounces) grated Gruyère or sharp white cheddar, divided

¾ cup heavy cream

½ cup low-sodium chicken broth

2 teaspoons chopped thyme (or 1 teaspoon dried)

1 teaspoon kosher salt

½ teaspoon ground black pepper

1. Heat oven to 375°F. Heat a skillet over medium-high heat and add couscous. Toast, stirring often, until golden brown in parts, about 4 minutes. Transfer to a 2-quart baking dish and spread evenly in the bottom.

2. To prepare cauliflower, steam in a stovetop steamer, or place cauliflower in a large microwave-safe bowl with a few tablespoons of water, cover, and microwave on high 6 to 8 minutes until just tender.

3. To the steamed cauliflower, add 1½ cups cheese, cream, broth, thyme, salt, and pepper. Toss to combine. Layer over couscous in the baking dish and top with remaining ½ cup cheese.

4. Bake until golden brown and bubbly and until cauliflower is slightly caramelized, 30 to 35 minutes. Serve hot.

NOTE Two pounds of cauliflower florets is about 8 cups. For easy preparation, you can buy bags of pre-cut florets.

crispy and spicy harissa potatoes with yogurt

AT MY HOUSE, unspoken-for potatoes immediately run the risk of being commandeered for this recipe. These buttery-soft potato bites are coated in a super simple sweet-and-savory crust that gets a little heat from harissa (a chili paste used in North African and Middle Eastern cooking). I typically have a red onion, nuts (pistachios are my favorite here), and herbs hanging around from other recipes, and they make for uncomplicated toppings that stick to the potatoes as they are dipped in creamy yogurt. If you need a new signature potato dish, might I suggest this gem!

These taters are absolutely delicious served with a big bowl of lightly dressed greens or arugula. Scoop potatoes and yogurt on top of each serving of greens for an entrée salad.

SERVES

6

HANDS-ON TIME

25 MINUTES

TOTAL TIME

1 HOUR 10 MINUTES

POTATOES

1½ pounds baby Yukon Gold or creamer potatoes

1 tablespoon kosher salt

HARISSA SAUCE

2 tablespoons harissa

3 tablespoons olive or avocado oil

1 tablespoon honey

2 cloves garlic, minced

HERB TOPPING AND YOGURT

2 tablespoons finely chopped red onion or shallot

5 tablespoons finely chopped pistachios

3 tablespoons chopped flat-leaf parsley

1 tablespoon chopped oregano

1¼ cups plain whole milk yogurt or Greek yogurt

1. Heat oven to 375°F. Line a baking sheet with nonstick foil, or use a nonstick baking sheet.

2. To parcook potatoes: In a medium saucepan, cover potatoes with water and add salt. Bring to a simmer and cook until just tender when checked with a fork, 10 to 12 minutes. Drain and set aside until cool enough to handle.

3. For the harissa sauce: In a large mixing bowl, whisk together all harissa sauce ingredients.

4. Once potatoes are cool, cut each in half, or cut large potatoes into 2-inch pieces. Transfer to mixing bowl with harissa mixture and toss to coat.

5. Transfer to prepared baking sheet. Roast until crispy and golden, about 30 minutes, turning potatoes over with tongs halfway through cooking.

6. While potatoes cook, prepare herb topping by combining red onion, pistachios, parsley, and oregano.

7. To serve, spoon yogurt on a serving platter and top with potatoes. Sprinkle on some herb mixture and serve extra on the side.

SERIOUS SIDES

117

SERVES

8 TO 10

MAKES

ABOUT 8 CUPS

TOTAL TIME

30 MINUTES

creamy garlic-and-herb mac and cheese

THIS IS A LUXURIOUSLY CREAMY stovetop mac and cheese that doesn't shy away from flavor. If you know that tasty Boursin cheese you buy at the store, you'll be familiar with my homemade version in this recipe. I've mixed cream cheese and those same herbs and seasonings into the pasta sauce, and they elevate your mac and cheese like nothing else!

The mix of Parmesan and white cheddar adds layers of flavor. You can change the intensity of this dish just by choosing an aged white cheddar with a stronger taste or by playing around with cheddars from different regions.

This mac is versatile too. Adding veggies or bacon creates an entirely new recipe with that same herby-cheese goodness. I love this served as a main dish with a salad on the side, as a side at a BBQ, with burgers off the grill, or next to roast chicken.

1 pound curly pasta, such as cavatappi

½ cup (4 ounces) cream cheese, room temperature

½ cup (2 ounces) finely grated Parmesan

½ teaspoon white pepper

2 tablespoons finely chopped flat-leaf parsley, plus more for topping

2 tablespoons finely chopped chives or scallions

1 teaspoon Dijon mustard

Pinch cayenne pepper

½ teaspoon garlic powder

1 teaspoon kosher salt

2 tablespoons butter

2 tablespoons all-purpose flour

2 cups whole milk

1¾ cups (7 ounces) grated white cheddar

1. Cook pasta in salted water according to package directions. Drain, rinse, and set aside.

2. While pasta cooks, mix together cream cheese, Parmesan, white pepper, parsley, chives, Dijon mustard, cayenne pepper, garlic powder, and salt. Stir with a wooden spoon or spatula until smooth. Set aside.

3. In the pasta pot or another large pot, melt butter over medium-high heat. Whisk in flour. Add milk and vigorously whisk to make sure there are no lumps. Continue whisking slowly until mixture just starts to boil and thickens.

4. Reduce heat to medium-low. Whisk in cream cheese mixture. Add white cheddar a handful at a time, stirring between each addition until cheese is melted.

5. Stir in pasta. Transfer to a serving dish and garnish with extra chopped parsley to serve.

SERIOUS SIDES

MAIN EVENTS

I usually plan my parties or dinner menus around a main dish, and I'd guess you often do as well. I like to plan the flavors and prep time required for that main dish before I start adding side dishes and desserts!

In my opinion, a main dish doesn't always need to be a big to-do. It could be a fun pasta, a comforting soup, or a sandwich. Try my grilled chicken sandwich for a weeknight dinner or casual gathering.

That being said, I'm also a big fan of making a meal the "main event" of your get-together. Those main events can be stellar dishes your crowd will *love*! I know you'll find new favorites in this chapter, like the mushroom and spinach risotto or the three-cheese and zucchini ravioli. For those times you want to really wow your dinner guests, try impressive dishes like a blackened salmon or giant meatballs.

In this chapter, I've shared tips for prepping ahead and entertaining as well as recipes you can master to make several meals—like a quick marinara, which is the start to three delicious main dishes, or the beef-and-bacon chili, which magically turns into chili cheese fries and chili con queso.

skirt steak with strawberry chimichurri and rice pilaf

THE VERSATILITY of this recipe knows no bounds. Fresh strawberries mixed into a traditional chimichurri sauce are fantastic in the summer, lending a sweet to the savory of the rest of the meal. But try other fresh fruit as the seasons allow. I'm talking mango, pineapple, grapes, or figs, all easily diced and added to the sauce just before serving.

I've used my super simple steak rub here (I use it on my Seasoned Grilled Steak, page 81) and paired it with an everyday staple, Buttery Rice Pilaf (page 113). Adding slivered, toasted almonds is a delightful extra.

SERVES

4 TO 6

HANDS-ON TIME

25 MINUTES

TOTAL TIME

35 MINUTES,
NOT INCLUDING
RICE PREPARATION

RICE

1 recipe Buttery Rice Pilaf with Vermicelli (page 113)

⅓ cup slivered almonds, toasted

STEAK

1¼ pounds skirt steak

1½ teaspoons ground cumin

1½ teaspoons kosher salt

CHIMICHURRI

½ cup finely chopped flat-leaf parsley

2 cloves garlic, minced

3 tablespoons finely chopped shallot or red onion

2 tablespoons chopped oregano

2 tablespoons finely chopped cilantro

2 tablespoons sherry vinegar or red wine vinegar

2 tablespoons fresh lemon juice

2 tablespoons honey

1 teaspoon kosher salt

½ teaspoon ground cumin

⅛ teaspoon cayenne pepper

⅓ cup extra-virgin olive oil

1 cup finely chopped strawberries

1. For the rice: Prepare rice pilaf and stir in slivered almonds. Set aside and keep warm.

2. For the steak: Heat grill to medium-high. Pat skirt steak dry with paper towels and thread it lengthwise onto two long skewers and keep it at an even thickness. Then rub steak all over with cumin and salt.

3. For the chimichurri: In a bowl combine all chimichurri ingredients except olive oil and strawberries. Stir in olive oil and set aside.

4. Grill steak to medium doneness, about 4 minutes per side. Let rest about 5 minutes.

5. Just before serving, stir strawberries into chimichurri. Serve steak over rice with strawberry chimichurri on top.

> **TARA'S TIP**
>
> Skirt steak is long and thin, so the cooking time is short. If you don't have an outdoor grill, it's also great cooked under a broiler or on a grill pan on the stove. Simply adjust your cooking time depending on how hot your broiler or pan is.
>
> You can use flank steak in place of skirt steak. Simply adjust your cooking time because flank steak is thicker.

MAKES

4 TO 6 SERVINGS,
6½ CUPS

HANDS-ON TIME

35 MINUTES

TOTAL TIME

55 MINUTES

italian gnocchi, bacon, and cheese soup

FLECKED WITH VEGGIES AND KALE, this creamy soup is my version of a delicious baked-potato soup, but I swapped the potato for gnocchi, a potato pasta! The soft, pillowy gnocchi melts in your mouth, and herbs and Parmesan fill your kitchen with classic Italian warmth. You're in for the coziest meal of the week with a bowl of this cheesy soup and some warm bread. (Try my Easy French Bread, page 110.)

Try my Easy French Bread, page 110.

TARA'S TIP

I throw a few extra strips of bacon in the pot to crisp and save them for garnish (if they escape sneaky nibbles before the soup is done).

Find prepared potato gnocchi vacuum-sealed in the pasta aisle or refrigerator section at the store. Don't use any type of dried gnocchi.

5 slices bacon, roughly chopped

1 tablespoon olive oil

1½ cups finely diced onion

½ cup diced carrot

½ cup diced celery

2 cloves garlic, minced

1 tablespoon chopped thyme (or 1 teaspoon dried)

1 teaspoon chopped rosemary (or ½ teaspoon dried)

⅛ teaspoon red pepper flakes

2 tablespoons all-purpose flour

4 cups chicken or vegetable broth

1 (16-ounce) package potato gnocchi

1 cup whole milk

½ cup (2 ounces) grated sharp white cheddar

¼ cup (1 ounce) finely grated Parmesan

3 cups roughly chopped kale, tough stems removed

Kosher salt

1. Heat a 4-to-6-quart Dutch oven or soup pot over medium heat. Add bacon and cook, stirring occasionally, until crisped, about 5 minutes. Remove bacon and set aside. Drain off all but 2 tablespoons of bacon grease.

2. Increase heat to medium-high. Add olive oil, onion, carrot, celery, and garlic to bacon grease. Cook until vegetables are softened, about 5 minutes.

3. Add thyme, rosemary, red pepper flakes, and flour. Stir to coat everything in flour, then add broth. Simmer, stirring occasionally, until vegetables are tender and broth has thickened slightly, 15 to 20 minutes.

4. Stir in gnocchi, milk, cheddar, Parmesan, and kale. Stir until soup is smooth and cheese is melted. Stir in bacon. The soup may simmer gently, but do not boil.

5. Season to taste with salt and serve. Garnish with extra bacon and herbs if desired.

NOTE Because of the starchy gnocchi, leftovers of this soup become very thick. Reheat with a little extra broth to acheive the consistency you like.

chicken banh mi burgers

A BANH MI is a traditional Vietnamese sandwich spread with pâté, and while that's a great flavor, I stick with a chicken burger for a crowd. Classic flavors of sriracha, mayo, and sesame add finishing touches. Use your favorite store-bought roll or rolls made from my Easy French Bread recipe (page 110).

The banh mi sandwich shops in New York let you choose your own toppings, so let your family or guests do the same. The standard fare is a mixture of pickled carrots, daikon radish, and cucumbers, but you can add chopped peanuts and extra cilantro or mint.

SERVES

4 TO 6

HANDS-ON TIME

40 MINUTES

TOTAL TIME

45 MINUTES

SESAME CHICKEN BURGERS

- 1 pound ground chicken
- 2 cloves garlic, minced
- ⅔ cup chopped cilantro
- 2 tablespoons finely diced jalapeño
- 1 teaspoon fish sauce
- 2 teaspoons grated fresh ginger
- 2 teaspoons sesame oil
- Canola or avocado oil for grilling

TOPPINGS

- 2 tablespoons rice wine vinegar
- 1½ teaspoons sesame oil
- 2 teaspoons granulated sugar
- ½ cup mayonnaise
- 2 teaspoons sriracha sauce
- ¾ cup shredded or julienned carrots
- ¾ cup julienned daikon radish
- 2 Persian cucumbers, thinly sliced
- 4 or 6 sandwich rolls
- ⅓ cup chopped peanuts
- ⅓ cup chopped cilantro or mint
- Lime wedges
- 1 small jalapeño, sliced (optional)

1. For the burgers: Line a baking sheet with parchment or prepare squares of parchment for layering. Set aside.

2. With gloved hands or a wooden spoon, thoroughly mix all burger ingredients except canola oil. Form mixture into 4 or 6 patties. Place patties on prepared baking sheet or layered between squares of parchment. Chill until ready to grill.

3. Heat a grill to medium-high. Alternatively, you can panfry the burgers in a nonstick skillet on a grill pan for about 4 minutes per side.

4. While the grill heats, prepare the toppings: Whisk together rice wine vinegar, sesame oil, and sugar until sugar is dissolved. In another bowl combine mayonnaise and sriracha. Stir 1 tablespoon vinegar mixture into sriracha mayo. Set aside. Just before serving, toss remaining vinegar mixture on vegetables (carrots, radish, cucumber).

5. Brush one side of each burger with canola oil and place that side on the hot grill. Cover and cook 3 minutes. Brush tops with canola oil and gently flip burgers. Cover and cook until done all the way through, about 3 minutes more.

6. Spread some sriracha mayo on each sandwich roll. Add a chicken burger, vegetables, and a sprinkling of peanuts and cilantro. Serve with limes for squeezing and jalapeños for extra heat, if desired.

TARA'S TIP

The chicken mixture for the burgers can be divided up in different ways. Make 4 large burgers (½ cup mixture each) for big eaters or 6 smaller burgers for regular appetites. You can also make small slider patties for a party and even meatballs that get cooked in the oven. Try serving meatballs and all the toppings over rice as a rice bowl or in a soft flatbread wrap.

MAKES

6 TO 8 SERVINGS,
10 CUPS BEANS

HANDS-ON TIME

25 MINUTES

TOTAL TIME

2 HOURS, NOT
INCLUDING
SOAKING TIME

red beans and rice with avocado salad

I HAD THE BEST rice and beans of my life at a food stand on the side of the road in Puerto Rico. We were driving through the rain forest and had miles to go before we hit the town on the other end, and we were starving. Grateful there was a little stand with a few chairs and a table on the side of the road, we took our chances, and thank goodness!

I've tried to re-create that meal for years, and this is spectacularly close to the original. It's going to go on your list of favorite comfort foods, I promise!

Caribbean households all have their own version of rice and beans. Some make it with *sofrito* and pink beans, others with kidney beans and diced veggies, like me. Serve it with soft rolls or crispy plantain *tostones* and Avocado Salad (page 109), but always over rice to soak up the stewy goodness.

I don't recommend using canned beans because you'll lose the layers of flavor. An Instant Pot can make things go faster.

TARA'S TIP

I love using a quick-soak method for beans when I forget to put them in water 6 hours in advance! In a large pot, cover beans with water and bring to a boil. Cover and remove from heat. Let sit 1 hour, then drain. Proceed with the recipe.

You can also prepare this meal in an Instant Pot. Soak and drain beans. Then cook beans with all dry bean ingredients and 5 to 6 cups water on high pressure for 10 minutes. Let pressure naturally release for at least 20 minutes. After removing cooked beans, you can continue the recipe from step 2 in the Instant Pot on sauté mode.

DRIED BEANS

1 (1-pound) bag red kidney beans, soaked 6 hours or overnight and drained

3 strips bacon

½ bunch cilantro, washed and tied with a string

½ red bell pepper, cut into pieces

½ teaspoon ground cumin

½ teaspoon kosher salt

RED BEANS AND RICE

3 strips bacon, cut into ½-inch pieces

1 medium yellow onion, diced

3 cloves garlic, minced

1½ red bell peppers, cut into ½-inch dice

1 green bell pepper, cut into ½-inch dice

½ teaspoon ground cumin

⅛ teaspoon cayenne

1 teaspoon chili powder

1 teaspoon dried oregano

1 teaspoon kosher salt

½ teaspoon ground black pepper

Pinch cinnamon

1 (28-ounce) can chopped tomatoes

1 tablespoon red wine vinegar

⅓ cup chopped cilantro

1½ cups uncooked converted rice, cooked according to package directions

Lime wedges

Avocado Salad (page 109)

1. In a large stockpot, combine all dried bean ingredients. Cover with water to an inch above the beans. Bring to a boil, then reduce heat and simmer until beans are tender, about 1 hour 15 minutes. Drain, reserving 3 cups cooking water. When beans are cool enough to handle, remove bacon strips, cilantro stems, and red pepper pieces and discard.

Continued on next page

2. While cooked beans cool, heat a 6-quart Dutch oven over medium heat. Add diced bacon and cook, stirring frequently, until cooked but not crisp, 5 to 7 minutes. Add onion and garlic and cook another 2 minutes.

3. Add bell peppers, cumin, cayenne, chili powder, oregano, salt, pepper, and cinnamon. Cook, stirring frequently, until peppers are soft and onions are translucent, 7 to 8 minutes.

4. Add tomatoes, cooked beans, and 2 cups reserved bean cooking water. Bring to a simmer and cook, stirring occasionally, until liquid has reduced and mixture becomes stewy, about 10 minutes. Add extra bean cooking water to create the consistency you want.

5. Stir in vinegar and chopped cilantro and season to taste with extra salt. Serve over rice with lime wedges for squeezing and avocado salad on the side.

quick marinara

WHIP UP THIS garlicky, tangy marinara sauce from basic pantry ingredients. I've used canned tomatoes because it cuts down on cooking time like crazy! The flavor is already concentrated. A generous amount of olive oil creates a nice silkiness, and adding plenty of garlic and dried or fresh herbs (depending on the season and what you have on hand) is really all you need for a flavorful sauce.

MAKES

2½ CUPS

HANDS-ON TIME

15 MINUTES

TOTAL TIME

40 MINUTES

¼ cup extra-virgin olive oil

4 large cloves garlic, sliced or minced

2 tablespoons chopped basil (or 2 teaspoons dried)

2 tablespoons chopped oregano (or 2 teaspoons dried)

1 (28-ounce) can petite diced tomatoes

½ teaspoon kosher salt

½ teaspoon ground black pepper

2 tablespoons chopped flat-leaf parsley (or 2 teaspoons dried)

1. Heat olive oil in a medium saucepan over medium heat. Add garlic and cook 1 minute.

2. Add basil, oregano, tomatoes, salt, and pepper. Cover and bring to a boil, then lower heat and simmer for 18 to 20 minutes. Stir in parsley just before serving.

3. Sauce can be used immediately or stored in the fridge for up to 5 days. Freeze for up to 2 months.

NOTE Double, or even triple, the recipe and store it for later to make "Creamy" Tomato and White Bean Soup (page 138), Three-Cheese and Zucchini Ravioli Pillows (page 142), or Giant Dinner Meatballs (page 141), or use it as a pizza sauce, pasta sauce, or topping for bruschetta.

pasta with brussels sprouts and walnut–sage browned butter

SERVES

4 TO 6

TOTAL TIME

45 MINUTES

THERE MAY NEVER BE a more delicious combination than this! Browned butter and sage put the Brussels sprouts into their own category of delightful pasta toppings. The crunchy nuts and savory onions complete this flavorful dinner with perfection.

While you could use any shape of pasta here, I really like twirling sturdy strands of fettuccine or tagliatelle around my fork so they catch the buttery sprout leaves.

½ pound fettuccine pasta

4 tablespoons butter

1 tablespoon olive oil

2 garlic cloves, minced

½ pound Brussels sprouts, leaves separated

¾ teaspoon kosher salt

¼ teaspoon ground black pepper

½ teaspoon finely chopped sage, plus leaves for garnish

¼ teaspoon chopped thyme

1 small red onion, sliced into thin wedges

½ cup grated Parmesan

⅔ cup chopped toasted walnuts

TARA'S TIP

To remove individual Brussels sprouts leaves, cut the stem out of each sprout with a paring knife or the small end of a melon baller and gently ease apart all the leaves. This process takes a few minutes, so it's a great task to prep ahead.

1. Cook pasta in very salty water according to package directions. Drain, reserving 1 cup pasta water. Set pasta and reserved cup pasta water aside.

2. Melt butter in a small saucepan over medium–high heat. Cook, stirring occasionally, until butter begins to brown and is very fragrant, 6 to 8 minutes. Don't strain. Set aside.

3. In a large skillet, heat olive oil over medium–high heat. Add garlic and cook until just fragrant, about 30 seconds. Add Brussels sprout leaves, salt, pepper, and herbs. Cook until leaves are bright green and softening, about 4 minutes. Add sliced onions and cook 1 minute more.

4. Add reserved pasta to skillet with Brussels sprouts and drizzle with browned butter, making sure to scrape in all the browned bits. Add reserved cup pasta water and Parmesan. Cook, stirring until everything is warmed through, seasoning with extra salt to taste. Serve garnished with walnuts.

NOTE To toast nuts like walnuts, cook them in a single layer on a baking sheet in a 350°F oven. Check them around 5 minutes, and if they aren't quite toasted and fragrant, leave them in for an additional 1 to 2 minutes.

MAKES

4 SANDWICHES

HANDS-ON TIME

20 MINUTES

TOTAL TIME

30 MINUTES

sweet-and-savory grilled chicken sandwich with bacon and pepper jelly

THIS SAVORY bacon and chicken sandwich touts melty cheese and sweet pepper jelly to make it a party-worthy winner. It's the titleholder as my mom's favorite sandwich, and why wouldn't it be with all those tasty flavors in one bite? Some crunchy chips and sparkling bevvies are all you need as accompaniments to this star of the show. This sandwich is great for a summer party, game night, or casual weekend gathering.

TARA'S TIP

The chicken can be grilled on an outdoor grill, in a grill pan on the stove, or on a panini press!

If you don't have cooked bacon ready to reheat (it disappears at my house), bake bacon on a foil-lined pan at 400°F for 12 to 15 minutes.

2 boneless, skinless chicken breasts (about 1¼ pounds)

1 teaspoon garlic salt

½ teaspoon ground black pepper

4 slices Havarti cheese

⅓ cup mayonnaise

⅓ cup pepper jelly

8 slices country white bread, toasted

8 slices bacon, cooked

2 cups baby arugula

1. Heat a grill or grill pan to medium-high. Cut chicken breasts in half horizontally to create 4 pieces. Place chicken between two sheets of plastic wrap and gently pound with a rolling pin to ¼-inch thickness. Season chicken on both sides with garlic salt and pepper. Grill until cooked through, 4 to 6 minutes total. Just before removing from grill, place a piece of cheese on each cutlet of chicken to melt a bit.

2. To make sandwiches, spread mayonnaise and pepper jelly on slices of toast, then layer with chicken, bacon, and arugula. Serve hot.

blue-ribbon beef-and-bacon chili

MAKES

4½ CUPS
WITHOUT BEANS

HANDS-ON TIME

35 MINUTES

TOTAL TIME

1 HOUR 10 MINUTES

DARE I SAY, this recipe will win you that chili cook-off blue ribbon! This chili con carne is the perfect topping for Chili Cheese Dogs (page 79), or you can add beans to make an all-around delicious bowl to eat with Golden Sweet Cornbread (page 88).

With just enough bacon to add some richness, this recipe has a great balance of roasted chilis and spices. The allspice is optional and could be swapped for a pinch of cinnamon if you like, but that little addition creates sweet warmth that's not overpowering. I'll bet you have almost all the ingredients in the pantry and spice cupboard.

1 Anaheim chili	1 teaspoon paprika
1 large jalapeño	¼ teaspoon allspice
4 slices bacon, finely chopped	1 tablespoon all-purpose flour
1 small onion, finely chopped	2 tomatoes from a can of whole tomatoes, crushed with your hands
2 cloves garlic, minced	1 (8-ounce) can tomato sauce (½ cup)
½ teaspoon kosher salt	1 (15-ounce) can beef broth
1 pound ground beef	1 (15-ounce) can drained kidney beans (optional if using for Chili Cheese Dogs, page 79)
1 bay leaf	
1 tablespoon chili powder	1 tablespoon red wine vinegar
1 tablespoon dried oregano	
1 teaspoon ground cumin	

> **TARA'S TIP**
>
> Extra chili can be used for Chili Cheese Fries (page 104) and the Ultimate Chili con Queso (page 107), so you might want to double the recipe while you're making it! Chili can be frozen up to 2 months and reheated.

1. To char Anaheim chili and jalapeño, heat broiler to high and arrange rack 4 to 6 inches from the heat. Place chili and jalapeño on a foil-lined baking sheet. Broil, turning occasionally, until chilis are charred and almost all black. Alternatively, cook directly over a gas stove burner.

2. Place charred chilis in a bowl and cover with plastic wrap. When cool enough to handle, remove and discard skin and seeds. Dice chilis and set aside.

3. In a 4-to-6-quart Dutch oven over medium heat, cook bacon, stirring frequently until fat is rendered and bacon is getting crisp, 5 to 7 minutes. Add onion, garlic, salt, and beef. Cook, breaking up beef into very small pieces, until beef is cooked through, 7 to 8 minutes.

4. Add roasted chilis, all remaining spices, and flour. Cook about 2 minutes. Add crushed tomatoes, tomato sauce, broth, and beans, if using. Bring to a simmer. Cover and simmer 20 minutes to meld the flavors. Add red wine vinegar and season to taste with salt. Serve with desired toppings.

NOTE If you're serving this as a bowl of chili, top with avocado, sour cream, grated cheese, scallions, or jalapeños.

MAKES

4 TO 6 SERVINGS,
5 CUPS

HANDS-ON TIME

20 MINUTES

TOTAL TIME

30 MINUTES,
NOT INCLUDING
MARINARA
PREPARATION

"creamy" tomato and white bean soup

THIS SILKY SOUP is creamy without any cream or milk. Canned white beans puréed with the homemade marinara create the texture of a cream-based tomato soup and thicken it at the same time. You'll love how comforting and rich-tasting it is with some croutons or a grilled cheese. The combo makes a cozy meal for a casual gathering or weeknight dinner.

GARLIC BREAD CROUTONS

4 slices rustic bread, diced

4 tablespoons butter, melted

2 tablespoons finely grated Parmesan

¼ teaspoon garlic powder

Pinch black pepper

SOUP

1 recipe (2½ cups) Quick Marinara (page 131)

1 (15-ounce) can white beans, drained

1 cup chicken or vegetable broth

½ cup roughly chopped basil

¼ teaspoon ground black pepper

1. For the croutons: Heat oven to 375°F. Line a baking sheet with foil. Toss all ingredients together, then transfer to prepared baking sheet. Bake until golden and crisped, 10 to 12 minutes.

2. For the soup: In a blender combine marinara, white beans, and broth. Blend until very smooth. Transfer to a pot and simmer 5 minutes, stirring occasionally.

3. Serve topped with basil, pepper, and croutons.

giant dinner meatballs

ONE OF MY FAVORITE Italian restaurants in New York serves fist-sized meatballs as an appetizer. They are so hearty and melt-in-your-mouth delicious that they, with the bread basket, usually act as my entire dinner. I'm sharing this idea with you and making it easy with my Quick Marinara (page 131). Plus, making giant-sized meatballs means less tedious rolling and fussing than with smaller ones, which means less hands-on time in the kitchen.

Serve with warm Easy French Bread (page 110) or salad. Either way, these meatballs make a perfect main dish for friends and family. *Mangia!*

---

3 cups chopped day-old white or French bread

1 cup whole milk

1½ pounds ground beef

½ pound sweet Italian sausage

1 large egg

4 cloves garlic, minced

1 cup finely chopped onion

1 medium carrot, minced

½ cup chopped flat-leaf parsley, plus more for garnish

1 teaspoon kosher salt

½ teaspoon ground black pepper

1 recipe (2½ cups) Quick Marinara (page 131)

1. Heat oven to 400°F. Line a baking sheet with foil. Set aside.
2. In a large mixing bowl, combine bread pieces and milk. Stir to coat, then let soak for 5 minutes.
3. Once bread has soaked, add all remaining ingredients except marinara. Mix until well combined, mashing soft bread pieces into the mixture.
4. Form mixture into 9 meatballs (about ⅔-cup mixture each). Place on prepared baking sheet. Bake until browned and firm, 25 to 30 minutes.
5. Transfer cooked meatballs to a 6-quart Dutch oven or stockpot with marinara. Bring to a simmer and cook 15 minutes. Serve meatballs with sauce and garnished with extra parsley.

MAKES

6 TO 8 SERVINGS, 9 LARGE MEATBALLS

HANDS-ON TIME

35 MINUTES

TOTAL TIME

1 HOUR 20 MINUTES, NOT INCLUDING MARINARA PREPARATION

TARA'S TIP

You can use plastic gloves while you mix all the meatball ingredients together to keep your hands clean.

If you have a food processor, you can make quick work of chopping the garlic, onion, and carrot. Cut them into pieces and process until they are all very finely chopped.

MAKES

4 TO 6 SERVINGS,
10 ZUCCHINI
PILLOWS

HANDS-ON TIME

40 MINUTES

TOTAL TIME

60 MINUTES,
NOT INCLUDING
MARINARA
PREPARATION

three-cheese and zucchini ravioli pillows

THESE PILLOWS ARE like ravioli with the zucchini playing the part of pasta. Thinly sliced zucchini ribbons are stuffed with a mixture of ricotta, Parmesan, mozzarella, and a generous amount of lemon zest. They get simmered in my garlicky Quick Marinara sauce (page 131) for a most amazing dinner.

To make the ravioli pillows, you'll need a mandoline (or awesome vegetable peeler) to slice the zucchini into ribbon strips, see page 169 for tips.

½ cup Panko breadcrumbs	1 tablespoon chopped basil (or ½ teaspoon dried)
1½ tablespoons butter, melted	½ teaspoon kosher salt
1½ cups whole-milk ricotta	½ teaspoon black pepper
½ cup grated Parmesan	3 medium zucchini (1½ pounds)
½ cup shredded mozzarella	1 recipe (2½ cups) Quick Marinara (page 131), warmed
1 tablespoon lemon zest	

TARA'S TIP

I use a small
2-tablespoon
ice-cream scoop
to transfer the
ricotta filling into
the zucchini strips.

For a delicious twist,
swap the mozzarella
for 5 ounces of soft
goat cheese. For a
pesto version, omit
the lemon zest and
stir ¼ cup prepared
pesto into the filling.

1. Heat oven to 400°F. Stir breadcrumbs with butter and spread on a small baking sheet. Toast in the oven until golden, about 8 minutes. Set aside.

2. In a mixing bowl, combine ricotta, Parmesan, mozzarella, lemon zest, basil, salt, and pepper. Set aside.

3. Trim stems and ends from zucchini. Slice zucchini into 40 thin, flexible strips on a mandoline or using a vegetable peeler. Wear a protective glove if using a mandoline.

4. On a cutting board, lay 4 slices zucchini so they overlap each other in the center (like a star or asterisk). Place 2 tablespoons ricotta filling in the center, then fold over zucchini ends, flipping the entire pillow over after the last strip so the ends are tucked underneath. Repeat with remaining zucchini and filling, making 10 pillows.

5. Spread warm marinara in the bottom of a 9-by-13-inch baking dish. Place pillows over marinara and sprinkle with toasted breadcrumbs.

6. Bake until heated through, 20 to 25 minutes. Garnish with extra basil if desired. Serve hot with pasta, bread, or salad.

Crisscross 2 strips of zucchini ribbons like a plus sign, then lay 2 more over the top like an X. The strips will look like a star or asterisk. A dollop of the cheese mixture goes in the center, and the strips are folded over the filling. Flip the pillow over to secure the loose ends.

spicy chorizo and tomato pasta

ITALIAN PASTA AND Mexican chorizo are not your typical combination—but I guarantee you won't complain. Chorizo is a spiced pork sausage. The Spanish version is typically smoked and cooked, but you'll want to use fresh Mexican chorizo here and cook it in the skillet yourself.

Earthy mushrooms add to the meatiness of the dish, while tomatoes and salty cotija cheese give it that savory bite. It's a skillet meal you'll want to serve to guests as well as put on rotation for weeknight dinners.

I used a fun, unstuffed version of cappelletti pasta, but you can use orecchiette as a perfect shape for catching all the flavorful bits.

12 ounces orecchiette pasta

2 tablespoons olive oil

8 ounces fresh chorizo sausage, casings (if any) removed

2 cloves garlic, minced

¼ cup chopped scallions, plus more for garnish

8 ounces baby bella or cremini mushrooms, cleaned and quartered

¼ teaspoon kosher salt

2 cups (1 pint) cherry tomatoes, sliced in half

¼ cup crumbled cotija cheese, plus more for garnish

1. Cook pasta in very salty water according to package directions. Drain, reserving 1 cup pasta water. Set aside.

2. While pasta cooks, heat olive oil in a large nonstick skillet over medium-high heat. Add sausage and garlic. Cook, breaking sausage into crumbles, until browned, about 5 minutes.

3. Add scallions, mushrooms, and salt. Cook, stirring, until mushrooms are soft, 4 to 5 minutes. Add tomatoes and cook another 2 minutes.

4. Add pasta and ½ cup reserved pasta cooking water to skillet. Stir in cheese, adding more pasta water as desired to create a thin sauce. Cook another 3 minutes.

5. When pasta is saucy, serve immediately, topped with more scallions and cheese.

> **TARA'S TIP**
>
> It's not the perfect swap, but if you can't readily find fresh chorizo, substitute it with spicy Italian sausage plus 1 teaspoon each paprika and chili powder, ½ teaspoon each garlic powder and ground cumin, and ¼ teaspoon each ground coriander, dried oregano, dried thyme, and onion powder.

SERVES

4 TO 6

HANDS-ON TIME

25 MINUTES

TOTAL TIME

35 MINUTES

mamma mia! red pepper and burrata burgers

DARE YOUR GUESTS to hold back their exuberant exclamations after the first bite of this burger. That's why it must be named "Mamma mia!" I've mixed piquant roasted red bell peppers, Italian sausage, and Parmesan into the patties for awesome flavor and then topped them with cream-filled burrata cheese. They are the ultimate drip-down-your-elbows cheeseburgers.

Make 4 large burgers or 6 smaller burgers depending on the appetites you're feeding!

2 cloves garlic, minced

⅔ cup mayonnaise

1 pound ground beef

4 ounces spicy Italian sausage, casings (if any) removed

¼ cup finely chopped jarred roasted red peppers

¾ teaspoon kosher salt

¼ cup grated Parmesan

4 to 6 brioche burger buns

2 cups baby arugula

2 plum tomatoes, sliced

2 small rounds burrata

Fresh basil leaves, for garnish

1. In a small bowl, stir together garlic and mayonnaise. Cover and refrigerate until ready to use.
2. Heat a grill or griddle to medium-high heat.
3. In a large bowl combine beef, sausage, roasted red peppers, salt, and Parmesan. Don't overmix. Form mixture into 4 (⅔ cup-sized) patties or 6 (½-cup-sized) patties and press to ¾-to-1-inch thickness.
4. Grill burgers, turning once, until just cooked through, about 7 minutes total.
5. To assemble burgers, spread garlic mayonnaise on the bottom of each bun and top with arugula. Add a grilled burger, then some slices of tomato. Cut burrata into pieces and add a few to the top of each burger, making sure to include the creamy center. Add bun tops and serve. You can garnish with fresh basil leaves or add some to the bun along with the arugula.

white pesto pasta with spicy broccoli

YOU MAY THINK I'm off my rocker telling you pesto can be white! Well, I've really taken liberties with the classic basil-based sauce and created a flavorful paste with some similar ingredients like Parmesan, garlic, and nuts. You'll completely forget about your allegiance to definitions once you taste my creamy ricotta version!

While this saucy pasta would be delightful with Italian sausage crumbles, I've seasoned roasted broccoli with sausage seasonings, and it is the bomb! This delicious vegetarian meal is perfect for a weeknight but also elegant enough for a dinner party.

SERVES

4 TO 6

HANDS-ON TIME

20 MINUTES

TOTAL TIME

40 MINUTES

SPICY BROCCOLI

- 1 pound broccoli cut into small florets (4 cups)
- 1 clove garlic, minced
- ⅛ teaspoon paprika
- ⅛ teaspoon red pepper flakes, plus more for garnish
- ¼ teaspoon crushed fennel seeds
- ¼ teaspoon kosher salt
- 3 tablespoons olive oil

WHITE PESTO PASTA

- 1 pound rigatoni
- ½ cup (2 ounces) toasted walnuts
- Zest of 1 lemon
- 1 clove garlic, minced
- 2 teaspoons chopped oregano (or 1 teaspoon dried)
- ½ cup (2 ounces) grated Parmesan
- 3 tablespoons olive oil
- 1 cup whole-milk ricotta
- ½ teaspoon kosher salt

TARA'S TIP

Utilize your hot oven by toasting the walnuts just before, or along with, the broccoli. Spread walnuts on a baking sheet and place on the rack below the broccoli. Toast for 4 to 5 minutes. Watch closely and remove them when they are fragrant so they don't burn.

1. Heat oven to 400°F. Toss all broccoli ingredients together. Spread out on a baking sheet and roast until just tender and charred in parts, about 20 minutes.

2. Meanwhile, while oven heats, bring very salty water to a boil for the pasta. Cook pasta according to package instructions. Drain, reserving 1 cup pasta water. Set aside.

3. In a food processor or blender, combine remaining pasta ingredients. Blend together until smooth, adding reserved pasta water a little at a time until a nice sauce is created (you may not need all the water).

4. Toss pasta with sauce and top with broccoli. Add extra red pepper flakes as a spicy garnish.

SERVES

4 TO 6

HANDS-ON TIME

45 MINUTES

TOTAL TIME

1 HOUR

wild mushroom and spinach risotto

YOU'RE NO STICK-IN-THE-MUD when you bring the fungi to the party. Joking aside, mushrooms, whether dried or fresh, add delicious umami richness to recipes, and everyone loves that! This flavor-packed saucy risotto is overflowing with bits of wild mushrooms and mushroom broth. The short-grain Arborio rice cooks into the essential creamy starchiness, and savories like onion, garlic, and shallots—plus classic Parmesan—round out this divine dinner.

I often use a mix of dried mushrooms I have in my pantry. You can use a medley for depth of flavor or just one of your favorites, including porcini, shiitake, morel, oyster, or chanterelle.

TARA'S TIP

You can make this dish with dried herbs (using half the amount of fresh that is called for), but the fresh herbs really make this risotto shine. In my opinion, it's worth it!

7½ cups low-sodium chicken broth

½ ounce dried mushrooms, rinsed

2 tablespoons butter

1 tablespoon olive oil

1 cup finely chopped yellow onion

⅓ cup finely chopped shallot or red onion

2 garlic cloves, minced

½ teaspoon kosher salt

1½ cups Arborio rice

½ tablespoon chopped marjoram or oregano, plus more for garnish

½ tablespoon chopped thyme, plus more for garnish

½ cup grated Parmesan, plus more for garnish

2½ ounces baby spinach (2 packed cups)

Salt and black pepper

1. To make the mushroom broth, heat chicken broth in a saucepan over medium-high heat until just simmering. Place dried mushrooms in a bowl or tea strainer. Pour half the broth over mushrooms. Cover and let sit 10 minutes until mushrooms are very soft. Strain, pouring the strained broth back into the saucepan and setting the soft mushrooms aside. Keep broth warm on low heat. When mushrooms are cool enough to handle, chop them into very small pieces and set aside.

2. Meanwhile, in a large saucepan over medium heat, add butter and oil. Stir in onion, shallot, garlic, and salt. Sauté until onion is tender, about 5 minutes. Add chopped mushrooms, rice, and herbs. Sauté 4 minutes.

3. Stir in ½ cup warm broth. Cook until liquid is absorbed, about 1 minute. Add an additional 1 cup broth and simmer, stirring often, until liquid is absorbed, 2 to 3 minutes. Continue to stir and add more broth, about a cup at a time, until rice is tender, about 30 minutes. Reduce heat if broth is absorbing faster than 2 to 3 minutes time. Along with the last cup of broth, stir in Parmesan and spinach and remove from heat. When spinach is wilted, season with salt and pepper to taste and serve immediately, garnished with more cheese and remaining herbs.

thai coconut chicken and rice noodle soup

MAKES

4 SERVINGS, 7 CUPS

HANDS-ON TIME

35 MINUTES

TOTAL TIME

55 MINUTES

THIS SOUP IS very versatile and very addicting. The warm curried coconut broth goes so well with chicken and rice noodles, but you can replace those with shrimp or just extra vegetables of your choice. This recipe is easy to double, and you can make it to suit any crowd; for vegetarians, use veggie broth and see the "Tara's Tip" about fish sauce. Adjust the heat with how many serrano chili slices you add!

Make as is for a weeknight meal. If serving at a gathering, create little nests of cooked noodles on the side that guests can add to their bowls as you serve—otherwise the noodles may get overcooked and soggy.

SOUP

- 4 cups low-sodium chicken broth
- ½ pound (8 ounces) boneless, skinless chicken breast, cut into 2-inch pieces
- 1 (14-ounce) can light coconut milk
- 2 teaspoons fish sauce
- ½ teaspoon kosher salt

- 2 teaspoons Thai red curry paste
- 2 teaspoons grated fresh ginger
- 1 clove garlic, minced
- 1 tablespoon brown sugar
- ½ red bell pepper, diced
- 4 ounces thin green beans (haricot vert), cut into 1-inch pieces

NOODLES AND TOPPINGS

- 4 ounces Thai vermicelli rice noodles
- 2 scallions, thinly sliced
- Lime wedges

- Cilantro
- Sliced serrano chilis (optional)

1. In a large saucepan over medium heat, combine chicken broth, chicken pieces, coconut milk, fish sauce, and salt. Bring to a simmer and cook until chicken is done, 10 minutes. Remove chicken and set aside.
2. To the broth add curry paste, ginger, garlic, and brown sugar. Shred chicken and add it back in. Then add bell pepper and haricot vert and simmer until vegetables are just tender, 6 to 8 minutes. Season broth with extra salt to taste.
3. In a separate pot, cook rice noodles according to package directions.
4. Divide noodles between bowls and serve soup over the top. Garnish with scallions, lime, cilantro, and sliced chilis.

TARA'S TIP

I often get asked if there is a replacement for fish sauce (it's a strong, smelly fermented sauce), and the answer is not really! If you're skeptical, I suggest just cutting the amount in half to start. Fish sauce imparts a very unique and authentic umami flavor that's not really fishy and is actually delicious in small amounts. Some people swap it for soy sauce. If you are vegetarian, I'll allow it this once!

NOTE Thai rice noodles only take a few minutes to cook. If overcooked, they become soft and soggy. Start heating the water for them while making the other parts of the recipe, but to ensure the noodles are perfectly done, don't start cooking them until step 3 as noted.

texas-style beef brisket at home

THE LONE STAR STATE is known for its Texas-sized servings of flavor-packed brisket with a tangy tomato sauce (usually kicked up a few notches with some heat). Now, I'm not the cowgirl to knock a famous pitmaster's smoked brisket off its high horse, but I am here to say you can turn this primal cut into tender goodness in your own kitchen. I've offered a grilled and smoked method below, but my go-to is New-York-apartment-style cooked-in-the-oven BBQ brisket!

I crank my dry rub up 10 notches, use a vinegar Mop Sauce to impart extra flavor, and serve this brisket with my Texsaucy BBQ Sauce and BBQ Baked Beans (page 87).

No matter what method you use, saddle up, because you're looking at a time commitment in order to give this tough cut of meat the low and slow cooking it needs to tenderize. The grill method will give you a little smoke flavor, but if you are die-hard and have your own smoker, then giddyup! Your brisket will be super authentic.

SERVES

10

HANDS-ON TIME

40 MINUTES

TOTAL TIME

UP TO 7 HOURS

BRISKET

1 (5-to-6-pound) beef brisket

Terrific Ten-Ingredient Rub (recipe below)

¾ cup Mop Sauce (recipe below)

Texsaucy BBQ Sauce (recipe below)

5 cups wood chips, soaked, for smoking (optional)

TERRIFIC TEN-INGREDIENT RUB

3½ teaspoons paprika

3½ teaspoons kosher salt

2½ teaspoons dry mustard

2½ teaspoons ground cumin

2½ teaspoons chili powder

1¼ teaspoons ground black pepper

1¼ teaspoons garlic powder

¾ teaspoon celery salt

¾ teaspoon cayenne pepper

3½ tablespoons light brown sugar

MOP SAUCE

½ cup water

1½ cups apple cider vinegar

½ teaspoon kosher salt

1 tablespoon brown sugar

½ teaspoon black pepper

¼ teaspoon cayenne

¼ teaspoon red pepper flakes

TEXSAUCY BBQ SAUCE

1¼ cups Mop Sauce

1 teaspoon Terrific Ten-Ingredient Rub

1 cup ketchup

3 tablespoons Worcestershire sauce

¼ cup honey

In the Oven

1. Let brisket stand at room temperature for 1 hour. Meanwhile, make the rub, Mop Sauce, and BBQ sauce by combining all ingredients for each recipe.

Continued on next page

> **TARA'S TIP**
>
> Buy ½ pound (or more) brisket per person you are serving. Plan for leftovers too because you'll want to use the extra to make Tex-Mex Brisket Tacos (page 55).
>
> For my recipe a grocery store cut of flat brisket will suffice. If smoking or doubling the recipe, look for a whole packer cut with the point and flat muscles, which will be anywhere from 10 to 14 pounds. Your cooking times will be almost double.

2. Use remaining rub (left from using 1 teaspoon in the BBQ sauce) to rub brisket all over. Place fat-side up in a disposable aluminum pan. Cover pan with foil.

3. Heat oven to 325°F. Bake brisket in covered pan 1 hour. Uncover brisket and gently baste with some of the ¾ cup Mop Sauce using a large pastry brush or mop brush. Cook uncovered, basting with Mop Sauce about every 45 minutes, until brisket is very tender, 3½ to 4 hours more.

4. Remove from oven, tent with foil, and let rest 15 to 30 minutes. Serve, thinly sliced against the grain, with Texsaucy BBQ Sauce.

On the Grill

1. Prepare brisket in an aluminum pan according to steps 1 and 2 above. Heat grill to medium-low (250°F). Place covered pan on grill away from the heat for indirect cooking. Cover grill and cook 1 hour.

2. Remove foil and discard. Baste brisket with Mop Sauce. Add soaked wood chips to the grill in a smoker box over direct heat or to the grill's built-in smoker box. Cover grill and cook brisket, basting every 45 minutes, until brisket is tender, 4½ to 5 hours more. (I remove the wood chips after about 90 minutes of smoking.)

3. Remove from grill, tent with foil, and let rest 15 to 30 minutes before serving. Serve, thinly sliced against the grain, with Texsaucy BBQ Sauce.

On the Smoker

1. Prepare brisket according to steps 1 and 2 above but place it directly on the smoker grates with a drip pan underneath instead of in an aluminum pan. You will not cover it. Set smoker to 180°F using indirect heat. Smoke for 3 hours, basting with Mop Sauce at the beginning of every hour.

2. Increase smoker temperature to 225°F and cook, occasionally basting with Mop Sauce, until internal temperature of brisket is 204°F on an instant-read thermometer, 5 to 6 hours more.

3. Remove from smoker, tent with foil, and let rest 15 to 30 minutes before serving. Serve, thinly sliced against the grain, with Texsaucy BBQ Sauce.

SERVES

8 TO 10

HANDS-ON TIME

25 MINUTES

TOTAL TIME

35 MINUTES

blackened salmon with mango-lime salsa

NOT ONLY DOES my blackening seasoning give my catch of the day a beautiful ebony crust, but the flavor is out of this world. It's the most crowd-pleasing way to prepare a whole salmon filet and goes with almost any topping or side dish—cue Grape and Feta Quinoa (page 91) or Buttery Rice Pilaf with Vermicelli (page 113).

I think you'll love the sweet, citrusy, quick mango-lime salsa with the subtly spicy blackened fish. And because there is always some variety of mango in season, you can serve this all year. If you do feel like changing it up, try pineapple or sweet oranges in place of the mango, or leave the salsa off altogether and serve the salmon with Sheet Pan Potatoes (page 64) and lemon wedges.

TARA'S TIP

I double the blackening seasoning and keep extra in the pantry; it comes in handy for smaller portions of salmon or when I'm making half a recipe of Blackened Salmon Tacos with Mangoes and Purple Slaw (page 45).

Have leftovers? Flake the pieces of cold salmon into Salmon and Arugula Pasta (page 161).

BLACKENING SEASONING AND SALMON

2 tablespoons smoked paprika

½ teaspoon cayenne

2 teaspoons garlic powder

1½ teaspoons dried oregano

1 teaspoon ground black pepper

2 teaspoons kosher salt

1 (2½-to-3-pound) whole salmon filet, skin on or skinless

MANGO-LIME SALSA

1 ripe mango, peeled and diced

1 tablespoon honey

2 limes, divided, plus more for serving

2 tablespoons chopped cilantro

1. For the salmon: Heat oven to 450°F. Line a baking sheet with foil and spray with cooking spray.
2. In a bowl or a jar, mix together all spices for blackening seasoning.
3. If salmon is skinless, rub 2 tablespoons seasoning on the top and 1 tablespoon on the underside. If the salmon still has the skin on, season just the top with 2 tablespoons seasoning. Place on prepared baking sheet and cook to medium doneness, about 8 minutes. Reserve any remaining blackening seasoning for another use.
4. For the salsa: Combine diced mango and honey in a mixing bowl. Supreme 1 lime by cutting off the peel and slicing each segment from the membrane. Coarsely chop lime segments and add them to the mangos. Squeeze 2 tablespoons lime juice from the second lime and add to the mixture. Stir in cilantro just before serving.
5. Serve salmon with mango-lime salsa and extra lime slices.

salmon and arugula pasta

A DINNER THAT is fresh but filling, flavorful and comforting—amazingly, a bowl of pasta can be all those things, especially with a few lovely ingredients like tangy goat cheese, juicy tomatoes, and savory salmon.

This pasta dish is a great alternative to a heavy cheese-and-marinara pasta meal when you're gathering a crowd, or it can be a delightful weeknight meal for the family. The hot pasta wilts the peppery arugula for a perfect warm salad and melts the goat cheese into a creamy sauce.

SERVES

5 TO 6

HANDS-ON TIME

15 MINUTES

TOTAL TIME

40 MINUTES

1½ pounds salmon filet

1 teaspoon ground coriander

1¼ teaspoons kosher salt, divided

Zest of 1 lemon, divided

4 tablespoons olive oil, divided

1 pound linguine pasta

2 cups (1 pint) grape tomatoes, cut in half

1 small shallot, thinly sliced root to tip

4 ounces soft goat cheese, crumbled, plus more for garnish

½ bag (2½ ounces) baby arugula

Ground black pepper

TARA'S TIP

Use fresh or frozen-thawed salmon filets for this recipe, or skip cooking the salmon if you have leftover Blackened Salmon (page 158) in the fridge! Add it to the recipe cold; the hot pasta will warm it.

1. Heat broiler to high and arrange rack 4 inches from heat. Line a baking sheet with foil and place salmon skin-side down.
2. Combine coriander, ¾ teaspoon salt, and half the lemon zest in a small bowl. Drizzle salmon with 1 tablespoon olive oil and rub with zest mixture.
3. Broil salmon 8 to 10 minutes for medium-well, less time for medium. Transfer pan to a rack to let cool slightly.
4. Meanwhile, bring a large pot of very salty water to a boil and cook pasta according to package directions. Drain and transfer to a large bowl.
5. Peel salmon from skin and flake into pasta in large pieces. Add remaining ½ teaspoon salt, remaining lemon zest, remaining 3 tablespoons olive oil, tomatoes, shallot, crumbled goat cheese, and arugula. Gently toss to combine. Serve with extra goat cheese and ground black pepper.

spicy honey-lime chicken

OH HEY! Just your works-for-everything, anytime, delicious chicken recipe here! I'm not kidding, you will come back to this marinade every week. A little smoky, a little spicy, a tad sweet and citrusy, with a splash of umami savoriness—it's the bomb!

This chicken is perfection grilled, or you can bake it, cut it up and make kebabs, or throw it in the slow cooker or Instant Pot for shredded chicken. And don't throw out that marinade! Simmer it into a sauce and drizzle it over your entire plate.

3 large chicken breasts (about 2¾ pounds)

½ cup fresh lime juice

¼ cup honey

1 chipotle chili in adobo, finely minced

2 teaspoons adobo sauce, from canned chipotle in adobo

½ teaspoon onion powder

½ teaspoon ground cumin

½ teaspoon kosher salt

1 tablespoon Worcestershire sauce

Cherry tomatoes, for serving (optional)

Fresh Green Salsa (page 52), for serving (optional)

1. Using a sharp knife, cut each chicken breast in half horizontally to create 6 thinner pieces. Place in a zip-top freezer bag or glass dish.
2. To create marinade, in a bowl, whisk together lime juice, honey, chipotle chili, adobo, onion powder, cumin, salt, and Worcestershire sauce. Pour over chicken. Cover and refrigerate for at least 1 hour or up to 4 hours.
3. Heat a grill or grill pan to medium heat. Remove chicken from marinade. If using marinade for a sauce, transfer it to a saucepan and simmer for 15 minutes.
4. Grill chicken until cooked through, about 4 minutes per side. Serve drizzled with marinade sauce and topped with tomatoes and green salsa.
5. For shredded chicken: No marinating needed. Place all ingredients in an Instant Pot with ¼ cup water. Cook on high pressure for 10 minutes. Let pressure release naturally for 10 minutes. When chicken is cool enough to handle, shred it into pieces. Simmer juices until reduced and thickened and strain before serving, if desired.

TARA'S TIP

Endless options! I serve this grilled chicken shredded in my Salsa Verde Chicken Enchiladas (page 164). Try it as is with Buttery Rice Pilaf with Vermicelli (page 113) or Creamy Garlic-and-Herb Mac and Cheese (page 118). You can even swap it for the pork in my Tacos Carnitas (page 48).

MAKES

8 TO 10 SERVINGS,
13 ENCHILADAS

HANDS-ON TIME

30 MINUTES

TOTAL TIME

1 HOUR, NOT
INCLUDING CHICKEN
PREPARATION

salsa verde chicken enchiladas

THANKS TO STORE-BOUGHT tomatillo salsa, you don't have to make a fancy enchilada sauce for this dinner. Some simple assembly and bake time is all it takes for a melty-cheese, saucy-goodness kind of gathering meal. With some tortilla chips, Loaded Guacamole Dip (page 100), or Pepper Jack Nacho Cheese (page 103), you'll be a shoo-in for "most memorable meal" award.

ENCHILADAS

1 recipe Spicy Honey-Lime Chicken
(page 162), prepared for shredding

13 corn tortillas

Avocado or canola oil

2 (16-ounce) jars salsa verde

2 cups (8 ounces) shredded Monterey
Jack cheese, divided

TOPPINGS

Jalapeños

Radishes

Fresh Green Salsa (page 52)

Chopped cilantro

1. Shred cooked chicken and set aside; you should have about 4 cups.
2. Heat a medium skillet over medium-high heat or heat an electric griddle. Brush both sides of each tortilla with a little oil and cook until soft and turning golden in parts. Set aside.
3. Heat oven to 350°F. Spread 1 cup salsa verde into the bottom of a 2-to-3-quart baking dish.
4. Pour remaining salsa verde into a shallow bowl. Dip each tortilla in salsa verde, then fill with a little cheese, shredded chicken, and a small spoonful of more salsa verde. Roll and place seam-side down in the baking dish. Save about ½ cup cheese for later.
5. If there is remaining salsa verde, pour it over the enchiladas. Cover dish with foil and bake 20 minutes. Uncover and sprinkle with reserved cheese. Cook another 10 to 15 minutes, until cheese has melted and enchiladas are heated through.
6. Serve topped with sliced jalapeños, radishes, green salsa, and cilantro, if desired.

TARA'S TIP

I love my Spicy Honey-Lime Chicken (page 162) in these enchiladas, but you can use any shredded chicken you have on hand or a rotisserie chicken from the store, saving you time to make side dishes!

greek chicken meatballs with lemon orzo and tzatziki

YOU'LL FEEL LIKE the immortal champion of dinner when you make this meal from the gods. It's a pretty simple spread to put together, especially if you are one to make the meatballs ahead of time (hello, double-batch-for-the-freezer!). Since the orzo can be served at room temperature and the salad and tzatziki can be made and kept in the fridge, you can do some pretty epic meal prep before your guests or family come around.

The meatballs are loaded with fun Greek flavors like lemon, dill, and tangy feta. And you'll think you've died and gone to Mount Olympus if you make the Super-Soft Pita Bread (page 16) to go with the tzatziki yogurt sauce!

For other meals, take note: the tzatziki sauce is great with fries, on sandwiches, for dipping veggies, or as a sauce on grilled meats and chicken.

MAKES

6 TO 8 SERVINGS, 33 MEATBALLS

HANDS-ON TIME

1 HOUR 10 MINUTES

TOTAL TIME

1 HOUR 30 MINUTES

TZATZIKI

- 1 Persian cucumber
- ½ teaspoon kosher salt
- 1 cup plain Greek yogurt
- 1 clove garlic, minced
- 2 tablespoons extra-virgin olive oil
- 1 tablespoon fresh lemon juice
- 3 tablespoons chopped dill or mint

RED WINE VINAIGRETTE

- ¼ cup red wine vinegar
- ⅓ cup extra-virgin olive oil
- 1 tablespoon honey
- ½ teaspoon dried oregano
- Pinch salt and pepper

GREEK SALAD

- 1 head romaine lettuce, coarsely chopped
- ¼ red onion, thinly sliced
- ½ cup kalamata olives, pitted
- 2 tomatoes, cut into 1-inch pieces
- 1 Persian cucumber, cut into half-moons
- ½ green bell pepper, cut into 1-inch pieces
- ½ cup crumbled feta cheese

MEATBALLS

- 1 (10-to-12-ounce) package frozen chopped spinach, thawed
- 1 pound ground chicken
- 1 cup finely chopped yellow onion
- 1 clove garlic, minced
- ⅓ cup plain breadcrumbs
- 1 large egg
- 1 teaspoon lemon zest
- 2 tablespoons fresh lemon juice
- 1 tablespoon chopped fresh dill (or 1 teaspoon dried)
- 1 teaspoon kosher salt
- ¼ teaspoon ground black pepper
- ¾ cup (3 ounces) finely crumbled feta cheese, plus more for serving

Continued on next page

TARA'S TIP

I use disposable gloves when I handle the spinach so it's not so cold on my hands!

Double the meatball recipe and freeze uncooked meatballs for another time. To cook later, thaw meatballs in the fridge for a few hours, then bake as usual, increasing baking time by 5 to 10 minutes.

MAIN EVENTS

LEMON ORZO

2 cups dry orzo

3 tablespoons fresh lemon juice

2 tablespoons extra-virgin olive oil

¼ teaspoon ground black pepper

Pita bread for serving

1. For the tzatziki: Grate cucumber and toss with salt to help extract excess water. Place in a sieve over a bowl and let drain about 20 minutes. Press gently to remove more water. Then stir together cucumber with remaining tzatziki ingredients. Cover and refrigerate for up to a day until ready to serve.

2. For the red wine vinaigrette: Whisk together all ingredients. Set aside.

3. For the salad: Combine all ingredients. Keep refrigerated until ready to serve. Toss with vinaigrette just before serving.

4. For the meatballs: Heat oven to 375°F. Line a baking sheet with foil. Set aside.

5. Squeeze thawed spinach dry in handfuls. Then mix squeezed spinach with remaining meatball ingredients except feta. Mix well (with gloved hands). Then gently mix in feta.

6. Form mixture into 33 (2-tablespoon-sized) meatballs. Place meatballs on prepared baking sheet. Bake until cooked through and just turning golden, 18 to 20 minutes.

7. For the orzo: Cook orzo in very salty water according to package directions. Drain and transfer to a bowl. While pasta is hot, toss with lemon juice, olive oil, and black pepper. Set aside, stirring occasionally, until ready to serve.

8. Serve meatballs with orzo, tzatziki, and salad with extra feta and pita bread on the side, if desired.

STAY SHARP TOOLS

Keep a variety of tools in your kitchen to slice, shave, and shred your food for recipes. A variety of knives, including serrated, will help you slice perfectly. Vegetable peelers can prep veggies or make long ribbons of carrots, cucumbers, or tender squash. Kitchen shears are strong enough to cut through chicken bones but handy for herbs, bacon, and other things. Use a pastry cutter to make strips of dough for decorative pies like my Maple Hazelnut Pie (page 247). Microplane graters make quick work of citrus zest, garlic, or Parmesan cheese. A mandoline should only be used with a protective glove, but is invaluable for making the perfect slices of radish and julienne cuts, or zucchini strips for my Three-Cheese and Zucchini Ravioli Pillows (page 142).

BREAKFAST AND BRUNCH

Some of my favorite food memories are of shared breakfasts with my family. Waking up to Grandma's pancakes on a weekend and Dad's hot cereal, or his hash browns on Christmas morning brings a flood of happy thoughts. But breakfast for me is also sitting at a New York City diner and sharing sides of home fries or taking visitors to the fancy brunch spot for the best waffles of their life! I've re-created these memories for you to share at home with recipes for granola pancakes, a hash brown breakfast bake, brûléed oatmeal, and cinnamon-sugar waffles with dulce de leche.

My New York experiences have enhanced my childhood breakfast memories and influenced this chapter. Chocolate-swirled babka and slices of iced lemon pound cake are staples in the city and make for the best holiday brunches, just like the make-ahead almond ricotta bread pudding, reminiscent of the decadent almond croissants at bakeries in my neighborhood.

The star of this morning show (wink!) is my new coconut cream sweet roll recipe. I've been working on this recipe for a while now, and I am so excited for you to try this divine sweet bread.

new york chocolate babka

LAYERS OF RICH yeasted dough are twisted, rolled, and folded around a luxurious chocolate-cinnamon filling to make the most indulgent loaf of goodness. Just one slice will send you right to heaven whether you serve it for brunch, dessert, or alongside your favorite hot bevvy.

Traditionally, babka is swirled with cinnamon, but chocolate is my favorite filling, and I've taken a note from the famous Breads Bakery in New York and added a schmear of Nutella to my chocolate center. The crunchy streusel topping adds a bakery-style flourish, but you can leave it off as a variation.

You'll want to follow my instructions for rolling and twisting the loaves to create the very classic caverns and swirls in the bread. After you've done it once, you'll repeat the method with ease on the next loaves. This recipe makes 3 large loaves, and if you're serving this bread at a big holiday gathering or gifting it, I suggest baking immediately. Otherwise, follow my instructions for freezing a few loaves for later.

MAKES

3 LARGE LOAVES

HANDS-ON TIME

45 MINUTES

TOTAL TIME

3 HOURS
30 MINUTES

TARA'S TIP

The babka can be prepared through step 11 and then wrapped and frozen, unbaked, for up to a month. When ready to bake, remove from freezer, let stand at room temperature for 5 hours, and bake according to recipe instructions.

BABKA DOUGH

1½ cups whole milk, warmed (105–115°F)

¾ cup granulated sugar

2 large eggs, room temperature

2 large egg yolks, room temperature

4½ teaspoons instant yeast

6 cups (768 g) all-purpose flour

1 teaspoon fine salt

1 cup (2 sticks) unsalted butter, cut into 1-inch pieces, room temperature

CHOCOLATE-CINNAMON FILLING

1 pound (16 ounces) semisweet chocolate, chopped

¾ cup granulated sugar

2 tablespoons ground cinnamon

½ cup (1 stick) unsalted butter, cut into small pieces

1½ cups Nutella

STREUSEL TOPPING

1 cup confectioners' sugar

¾ cup all-purpose flour

½ cup (1 stick) unsalted butter, room temperature

1 large egg

1 tablespoon water

1. For the dough: In a bowl, whisk together milk, sugar, eggs, and egg yolks.

2. In the bowl of an electric mixer fitted with a dough hook, combine yeast, flour, and salt. Add egg mixture and beat on low speed until almost all the flour is incorporated, about 1 minute. Add butter and mix on medium speed until flour mixture and butter are completely incorporated and a soft, smooth dough forms, about 10 minutes. Dough will be slightly sticky when squeezed.

Continued on next page

3. Transfer dough to a large greased bowl. Cover with plastic wrap and set aside in a warm place to rise until it doubles in bulk, about 1 hour.

4. For the chocolate-cinnamon filling: In a food processor, pulse together chocolate, sugar, and cinnamon until finely ground. Add cold butter pieces and pulse until combined well but rough and crumbly. Set aside in the fridge.

5. For the streusel topping, using a mixer fitted with the paddle attachment, combine confectioners' sugar, flour, and butter. Mix until butter is incorporated and mixture is a crumbly dough. Cover and refrigerate until ready to use.

6. In a bowl, beat together egg and water for an egg wash. Set aside.

7. Generously butter three 9-by-5-by-2¾-inch loaf pans and line them with parchment, leaving two sides overhanging (see page 221 for example).

8. Gently punch down dough and divide into three equal pieces. Cover and let rest 5 minutes. Keep two pieces covered with plastic wrap or a bowl while you form one loaf.

9. On a clean work surface, roll dough into a 14-by-14-inch square. Spread ½ cup Nutella over the surface of the dough, leaving a 1-inch border. Brush edges with egg wash. Crumble a scant 2 cups of the chocolate filling evenly over Nutella.

10. Roll dough up tightly into a log. Pinch ends together to seal. Twist the entire roll 4 or 5 turns. Then brush the top of the roll with egg wash. Cover half of the top with about 2 tablespoons chocolate filling, then fold the other half of the roll over that filling. Pinch the ends to seal together. Twist this doubled roll about 2 turns, then fit into one of the prepared pans.

11. Repeat steps 9 and 10 with the other pieces of dough.

12. Heat oven to 350°F. Brush the top of the loaves with egg wash and crumble a third of the streusel topping over each loaf (if using). Loosely cover each pan with plastic wrap and let stand in a warm place for a second proof, 40 minutes.

13. Bake loaves, switching placement of pans halfway through (to avoid oven hot spots), until golden, about 50 minutes.

14. Lower oven temperature to 325°F. Bake until babka is a rich brown in color and cooked through, 15 minutes more. If your oven runs hot, check the loaves earlier. Cover loaves with foil if streusel is getting too brown.

15. Remove from oven to wire racks and cool 10 minutes. Remove loaves from pans and cool completely before serving. Baked and cooled babkas can be wrapped well and frozen up to a month.

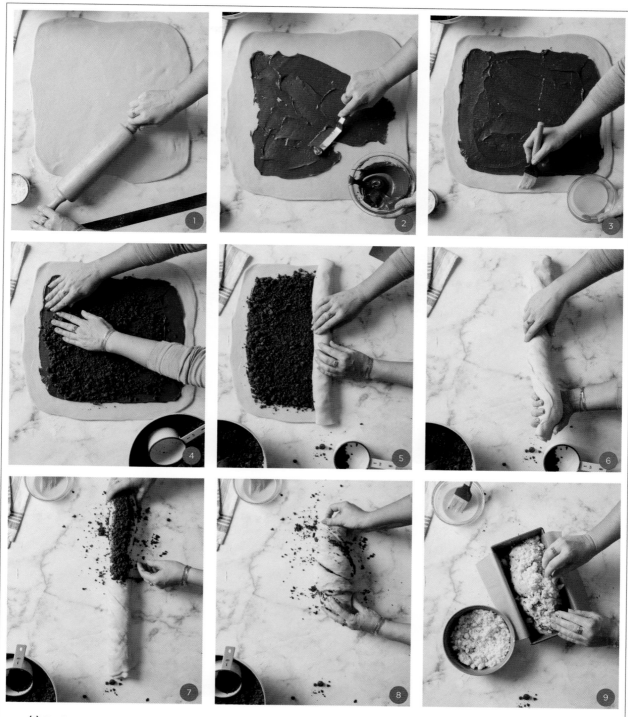

(1) Roll the dough into a square and (2) spread on Nutella, leaving a border. (3) Egg wash the border, (4) then sprinkle chocolate filling over Nutella. (5) Roll into a log and seal edges, (6) then twist the roll. (7) Sprinkle the roll with more filling, (8) then fold in half and twist again to fit in pan. (9) Sprinkle with streusel, proof, and bake.

half-and-half granola pancakes with ginger maple cream syrup

WITH GREAT PANCAKE MIXES on the store shelves, we don't often make pancakes from scratch anymore, but after enjoying these hotcakes, you may never go back to a mix again! A blend of half whole wheat and half all-purpose flour makes these pancakes rich and nutty and light and fluffy all at the same time. Adding bits of crunchy granola creates a breakfast worthy of my favorite NYC brunch spots!

To make this breakfast delicious enough for a holiday or special occasion, I add a generous drizzle of a creamy ginger maple syrup. It's so good!

GINGER MAPLE CREAM SYRUP

¾ cup pure maple syrup

¾ teaspoon freshly grated ginger

¾ cup heavy cream

PANCAKES

¾ cup whole wheat flour

¾ cup all-purpose flour

2 tablespoons light brown sugar

1 tablespoon baking powder

½ teaspoon fine salt

4 tablespoons (½ stick) melted butter

1½ cups milk, warmed

1 large egg

1 teaspoon vanilla extract

1¼ cups granola, crumbled

Fresh fruit and berries

> **TARA'S TIP**
>
> Keep this as your go-to recipe or make these swaps for the granola:
>
> **Banana Nut**
> 1¾ cups sliced banana and ½ cup finely chopped pecans
>
> **Berry**
> 2 cups blueberries or raspberries
>
> **Chocolate Chip**
> ¾ cup mini chocolate chips

1. For the syrup: In a small saucepan over medium-high heat, stir together all syrup ingredients. Stir until mixture is simmering, then remove from heat. Let cool slightly to serve with pancakes. Syrup can be stored chilled for up to a week. Reheat and whisk to serve.

2. For the pancakes: In a mixing bowl, whisk together flours, brown sugar, baking powder, and salt.

3. In a separate bowl, whisk together melted butter, milk, egg, and vanilla. Stir milk mixture into dry ingredients and combine until just mixed and only small clumps of flour remain. Do not overmix.

4. Heat a griddle or large skillet over medium heat. Brush the surface with extra butter.

5. Sprinkle griddle surface where you are going to place the pancakes with a bit of granola. Scoop about ¼ cup batter onto the griddle over the granola. Gently spread into a 4-inch circle and immediately sprinkle with a little more granola. When the bubbles on top pop and stay open, flip the pancakes and cook about 2 minutes more. Repeat for all pancakes.

6. If needed, keep pancakes hot in a warm oven while the others cook. Serve with syrup and fresh fruit.

diner breakfast potatoes

THERE IS SOMETHING MAGICAL about the potatoes served in New York City diners. You know the ones—the savory spiced morsels crisped on a hot flattop. They are the best accompaniment to any breakfast. You name it: pancakes, French toast, fried eggs, an omelet—all are made even more delicious with melt-in-your-mouth home fries on the side.

My method of parcooking the potatoes before crisping takes only a few minutes and softens them so they are buttery smooth on the inside and so the outside can brown to perfection. I make it easy and give you stovetop or oven directions.

MAKES

10 TO 12 SERVINGS,
9 CUPS

HANDS-ON TIME

25 MINUTES

TOTAL TIME

45 MINUTES

SPICE MIXTURE

1 teaspoon garlic powder

1 teaspoon ground coriander

½ teaspoon smoked paprika

1 teaspoon mustard powder

2½ teaspoons kosher salt

1 teaspoon ground black pepper

POTATOES

3 pounds russet potatoes, washed or peeled

1 medium yellow onion, diced

1 small red bell pepper, seeded and diced

1 small green bell pepper, seeded and diced

⅓ cup canola or avocado oil

TARA'S TIP

For a smaller gathering, simply halve the recipe and cook it in one skillet. I like to use the oven method for a big, full batch.

1. For the spice mixture: In a small bowl, mix together all spice ingredients.

2. For the potatoes: Cut potatoes into ½- to ¾-inch pieces (you'll have about 8 cups of diced potatoes). Transfer to a large pot and cover with water about 1 inch above the potatoes. Add a sprinkle of salt. Place over high heat and bring to a boil. Once boiling, reduce heat to a simmer and cook until potatoes are just getting tender but not soft, 8 to 10 minutes. Drain in a colander and rinse.

3. Toss parcooked potatoes with onion, bell peppers, oil, and spice mixture.

4. Skillet method: Heat two large nonstick skillets over medium-high heat. Add half the potato mixture to each hot skillet. Cook until onions are soft and translucent, stirring only occasionally to allow the potatoes to crisp, 6 to 8 minutes. Adjust heat as necessary to prevent burning or overbrowning.

5. Oven method: Heat oven to 425°F. Spread potato mixture evenly on a rimmed baking sheet. Roast until vegetables are soft and potatoes are crisped and golden, stirring once about halfway through cooking, 35 to 40 minutes total.

MAKES

4 SERVINGS,
2¾ CUPS

HANDS-ON TIME

15 MINUTES

TOTAL TIME

30 MINUTES

brûléed oatmeal

THIS INDULGENT hot cereal is a splendid spin on the most humble of breakfasts. If you like crème brûlée, you will totally be into the crackly layer of "burnt" sugar on top of my vanilla-infused oats. And even better: no torch needed! I make shards of glassy sugar in the oven so you can top several bowls of oatmeal at once. Serve with creamy whole milk and seasonal fresh fruit.

BRÛLÉED TOPPING

¼ cup granulated sugar

OATMEAL

2½ cups water

¼ teaspoon kosher salt

1 teaspoon vanilla extract

2 tablespoons brown sugar

1¼ cups rolled oats

Milk for serving

Fruit for serving

1. For the topping: Heat oven to 375°F. Line a baking sheet with a silicone baking mat or nonstick foil. Sprinkle sugar on baking sheet in a thin layer (forming a rectangle approximately 8-by-13 inches in size). Bake until melted and golden in color, 12 to 15 minutes. Let cool on pan on a wire rack. Once cool, break into pieces or shards.

2. For the oatmeal: Bring water, salt, vanilla, and brown sugar to a boil in a large saucepan over medium-high heat. Stir in oats. Let simmer 1 to 2 minutes. Reduce heat to low and cover. Let oats cook, covered, until tender and almost all liquid is absorbed, about 10 minutes more. Remove from heat and let rest 5 minutes, covered, before serving.

3. Divide oatmeal between 4 bowls. Add milk and fruit and top with desired amount of sugar shards.

family breakfast turnover

IT IS SO EASY to fill flaky puff pastry with a mixture of sautéed mushrooms, cheesy eggs, and ham for a terrific family-style breakfast. Slices of this savory turnover are perfect served with fresh fruit or a bowl of hot cereal. Make a few if you are serving a crowd or sharing on a brunch buffet, or make one for your family on a holiday morning.

Play around with your own combos for the filling—try different cheeses, vegetables, and herbs.

SERVES

4 TO 6

HANDS-ON TIME

25 MINUTES

TOTAL TIME

1 HOUR 20 MINUTES

2 tablespoons olive oil

2 cups (8 ounce package) sliced mushrooms

1 teaspoon thyme leaves (or ½ teaspoon dried)

2 large eggs, divided

⅛ teaspoon kosher salt

¼ teaspoon ground black pepper

1 cup (4 ounces) grated Fontina cheese

1 sheet puff pastry from a 17-ounce box, thawed if frozen

4 ounces sliced Black Forest ham

1. In a medium skillet, heat olive oil over medium-high heat. Add mushrooms and sauté until golden, 6 to 7 minutes. Add thyme. Set aside.

2. Heat oven to 375°F with rack in the lower third. Line a baking sheet with parchment.

3. In a bowl, mix together 1 egg, salt, pepper, and cheese.

4. On a floured work surface, roll pastry sheet into an 11-by-11-inch square. Place it on the prepared baking sheet. On half the dough, layer half the ham, leaving a 1-inch border. Add mushrooms, egg mixture, and another layer of ham.

5. Beat remaining egg. Brush border of pastry with some of the beaten egg. Fold dough over filling and press to seal edges. Use fork tines to make a design if desired. If pastry is room temperature, chill 20 minutes or freeze 10 minutes. If it is cool, skip that step and move on to baking.

6. Trim edges if necessary and brush entire pastry with some of the remaining beaten egg. Cut 3 vents on top of pastry. Bake, rotating once, until crust is golden brown and puffed, 35 to 40 minutes.

7. Transfer turnover on parchment to a rack to cool 10 minutes, then serve.

SERVES

6 TO 8

MAKES

8 SMALL WAFFLES

HANDS-ON TIME

35 MINUTES

TOTAL TIME

50 MINUTES

churro waffles with whipped ricotta and dulce de leche

A DUSTING OF cinnamon and sugar makes a delicious crust on these waffles, turning them into a churro-like treat. Topped with a dollop of not-too-sweet fluffy ricotta and drizzled with a caramelly sauce, this dish will transport you to breakfast paradise.

I add a splash of vinegar and use both shortening and butter in my waffles. All of these ingredients you likely already have in your pantry, and these additions make a big difference. Vinegar acts as a tenderizer; the acid makes each bite soft and brings out the taste of the other ingredients. The combination of fats ensures you get the flavor of butter and the soft cakeyness of shortening.

TARA'S TIP

These waffles have a light, crispy outside and soft inside like classic buttermilk waffles. You can swap the milk and vinegar for 1¾ cups buttermilk if you'd like.

Make this a fun dessert by swapping the ricotta cream for vanilla ice cream. Top with colored sprinkles!

RICOTTA CREAM

1¾ cups (15 ounces) whole-milk ricotta	2 tablespoons granulated sugar
½ teaspoon vanilla extract	

DULCE DE LECHE DRIZZLE

1 cup dulce de leche	¼ cup whole milk

WAFFLES

4 tablespoons butter	1¾ cups (224 g) all-purpose flour
4 tablespoons shortening	2 teaspoons baking powder
1¾ cups whole milk	1 teaspoon baking soda
1 teaspoon apple cider vinegar	1 teaspoon fine salt
2 large eggs	1 cup granulated sugar
2 teaspoons vanilla extract	1 tablespoon cinnamon

1. For the ricotta cream: In a food processor, combine all ricotta cream ingredients. Blend until very smooth, about 1 minute. Remove to a bowl and refrigerate.

2. For the dulce de leche drizzle: In a saucepan on the stove or in a microwave-safe bowl in the microwave, heat dulce de leche and milk until warm, stirring occasionally to thin the consistency to a syrup. Set aside and keep warm.

3. For the waffles: In a bowl in the microwave, melt the butter and shortening into the milk until milk is warm. Whisk in vinegar, eggs, and vanilla extract.

4. In a separate bowl, whisk together flour, baking powder, baking soda, and salt. Combine milk mixture and flour mixture and whisk until just mixed. Let rest while you heat a waffle iron.

5. Combine sugar and cinnamon in a large shallow dish or quarter-sheet pan.

6. Depending on your waffle maker, add just enough batter to fill the holes but not overflow. Cook until the outside is deep golden brown. Remove and immediately coat with cinnamon sugar by flipping it in the shallow bowl, gently pressing each side into the cinnamon sugar.

7. Serve waffles topped with ricotta cream and drizzled with dulce de leche syrup.

easy hash brown breakfast bake

YOUR ROSTER OF breakfast casserole recipes can be tossed aside. This has all the best parts of breakfast in one bite. My version is completely customizable—just use the hash brown egg base as your starting point, then add cheese, a little breakfast meat, and some veggies. The dollop of sour cream keeps the entire breakfast bake smooth and lush.

Assemble this the night before, keep it in the fridge, and bake it the next morning.

SERVES

12 TO 14

MAKES

1 (9-BY-13-INCH) CASSEROLE

HANDS-ON TIME

25 MINUTES

TOTAL TIME

1 HOUR 30 MINUTES

EASY HASH BROWN EGG BASE

1 tablespoon canola or avocado oil

1 medium yellow onion, finely diced

10 large eggs

1½ cups milk

½ cup sour cream

½ teaspoon kosher salt

½ teaspoon garlic powder

½ teaspoon dry mustard powder

1 (20-ounce bag) frozen shredded hash browns

BACON AND GRUYÈRE FILLING

1 pound bacon, cut into ½-inch pieces

2 cloves garlic, minced

5 ounces (about 5 cups) baby spinach

½ teaspoon ground black pepper

1 teaspoon dried thyme

1½ cups (6 ounces) shredded Gruyère cheese

¾ cup (3 ounces) shredded Fontina cheese

> **TARA'S TIP**
>
> The breakfast bake can be assembled, covered, and stored in the fridge overnight. Let sit at room temperature for 20 minutes before baking (while the oven heats).
>
> To halve this recipe, simply divide the ingredients in half and bake in a 8-by8-inch (3-quart) baking dish for about 35 minutes.

1. Heat oven to 375°F. Grease a 9-by-13-inch baking dish (or a 5-quart baking dish) with cooking spray and set aside.

2. For the hash brown egg base: Heat oil in a large nonstick skillet over medium heat. Add onion and cook until soft, 4 to 5 minutes. Set aside in a bowl.

3. In a large mixing bowl, whisk eggs until well beaten. Whisk in milk, sour cream, salt, garlic powder, and mustard powder. Add cooked onions and frozen hash browns and gently mix. Set aside while you prepare the filling.

4. For the filling: In the same skillet over medium heat, cook bacon, stirring, until just crisped, 5 to 6 minutes. Remove from heat and stir in garlic, spinach, pepper, and thyme. When spinach is almost wilted, add bacon mixture to the egg mixture with almost all of the cheese, reserving some for the top.

5. Pour mixture into baking dish and top with reserved cheese. Bake until the top is light golden and a knife inserted in the middle comes out clean, about 45 minutes. Let cool for 5 minutes before serving.

NOTE For variations, add these ingredients into the hash brown base.

Cheddar, Scallions, and Ham: 1½ cups diced cooked ham, ½ cup sliced scallions, ½ teaspoon ground black pepper, ¼ cup chopped flat-leaf parsley, 2 cups shredded cheddar cheese.

Chorizo Black Bean: 1½ cups cooked chorizo sausage, ¾ cup canned black beans, 1 cup diced and cooked red bell pepper, ½ teaspoon cumin, ½ teaspoon chili powder, 2 cups shredded Monterey Jack cheese.

Sausage and Mushroom: 1 pound cooked sweet Italian sausage, 1 teaspoon dried thyme, 8 ounces sliced mushrooms, sautéed, ¼ cup grated Parmesan, 1½ cups shredded Swiss cheese.

SERVES

8 TO 10

HANDS-ON TIME

50 MINUTES

TOTAL TIME

5 HOURS

cinnamon-sugar, almond, and ricotta bread pudding

LUSCIOUS POCKETS of cinnamon sugar, candied almonds, and sweet ricotta are swirled inside this custardy bread pudding. It's so good with fresh berries, a berry sauce, or maple syrup that you will be making it on the regular.

The simple candied nuts can be made days in advance. Unless this is for a late-morning brunch, you'll want to prepare the entire pudding the night before so it can rest and soak up all the custardy goodness before baking it in the morning.

Any soft bread or brioche will work, but if you've got it made, use my Easy French Bread (page 110) for a gorgeous texture.

CANDIED ALMONDS

6 ounces (2 cups) sliced almonds

¼ teaspoon cinnamon

¼ teaspoon fine salt

6 tablespoons granulated sugar

1 large egg white

¼ teaspoon vanilla extract

2 teaspoons water

RICOTTA CREAM

½ cup whole-milk ricotta

3 ounces cream cheese, softened

1½ tablespoons granulated sugar

½ teaspoon vanilla extract

BREAD PUDDING

Butter for dish

¾ loaf (about 15 ounces) soft French bread or brioche

7 large eggs

2 cups whole milk

9 tablespoons granulated sugar, divided

1 teaspoon cinnamon

Berries and syrup for serving

1. For the candied almonds: Heat oven to 275°F. Line a baking sheet with parchment.

2. In a mixing bowl, combine almonds and cinnamon. In a different bowl, whisk together salt, sugar, egg white, vanilla, and water until very foamy and almost forming soft peaks, about 2 minutes. Stir together almond mixture and egg white mixture.

3. Spread almonds evenly on prepared baking sheet. Bake until light golden, 30 minutes, gently tossing almonds with a spatula halfway through. Let cool.

4. For the ricotta cream: With a hand mixer, blend together all ricotta cream ingredients. Set aside.

5. For the bread pudding: Butter a 3-to-4-quart baking dish. Set aside.

6. Cut bread into ¼-inch-thick slices, and then cut the slices into quarters.

7. In a very large bowl, whisk eggs. Add milk and 7 tablespoons sugar. Whisk to combine well.

Continued on next page

8. Gently add half the sliced bread to the egg mixture to soak through. Immediately layer the soaked slices in the buttered dish, overlapping slices to fill the dish. Dollop half the ricotta cream in spoonfuls in various places over the bread, then sprinkle with ½ cup candied almonds. Layer with remaining bread dipped in egg mixture. Pour any leftover egg mixture over the layers in the dish, then dollop on remaining ricotta cream and sprinkle with another ½ cup candied almonds.

9. Cover dish with plastic wrap and chill 4 hours or overnight.

10. When ready to bake, heat oven to 350°F. Combine remaining 2 tablespoons sugar with cinnamon and sprinkle over the top of bread pudding. Bake until eggs are set and top is golden, about 45 minutes. Cover with foil during last 10 minutes if top is getting too brown. Serve with berries and syrup.

coconut cream sweet rolls

THIS SWEET ROLL has had many iterations, but I landed on what I describe as a coconut cream roll. A custardy coconut mixture is rolled inside a delicious dough, then a melt-in-your-mouth cream-cheese coconut buttercream is slathered on top. It's heavenly!

These rolls are perfect for breakfast or dessert, a spring or Easter event, or a New Year's brunch. I love them served with loads of fresh berries at a summer cookout.

I use my super soft cinnamon roll dough from TaraTeaspoon.com. The dough is unbelievably silky and pillowy tender, and it stays fresh-tasting for days after being baked. I use a method that calls for cooking flour and liquid into a pudding-like paste before adding it to the dough. This paste, referred to in the food world as *tangzhong*, is the base of many Asian-style breads and helps the dough retain moisture and not dry out.

MAKES

15 MEDIUM ROLLS

HANDS-ON TIME

45 MINUTES

TOTAL TIME

3 HOURS

TANGZHONG STARTER

5 tablespoons water

5 tablespoons whole milk

3 tablespoons all-purpose flour

ROLL DOUGH

4 cups (512 g) all-purpose flour

1¾ teaspoons fine salt

1 tablespoon instant yeast

¼ cup nonfat dry milk powder

¾ cup whole milk, warmed (95–105°F)

2 large eggs, room temperature

6 tablespoons unsalted butter, melted

COCONUT CREAM FILLING

1¼ cups granulated sugar

½ teaspoon fine salt

3 large egg yolks

1 (13.5-ounce) can coconut milk

½ cup (1 stick) unsalted butter

1 teaspoon coconut extract

2½ cups (7 ounces) sweetened shredded coconut, lightly toasted (see Tara's Tip)

COCONUT CREAM-CHEESE BUTTERCREAM

½ cup (1 stick) unsalted butter, softened

4 ounces cream cheese, softened

Pinch fine salt

1 teaspoon coconut extract

2½ cups confectioners' sugar

Toasted coconut, for garnish

> ### TARA'S TIP
>
> Toast coconut by spreading it evenly on a baking sheet and cooking in a 350°F oven for 6 to 8 minutes. Stir it once or twice because some coconut will brown more quickly if there are hot spots in the oven. Not every piece will toast, but most will get a nice light-brown color. Watch it closely the last minute or two—it goes fast at the end!

1. For the tangzhong: In a small saucepan over medium heat, combine all tangzhong ingredients. Whisk together and cook, stirring, until mixture thickens, 3 to 4 minutes. The mixture will be the consistency of thick pudding. Remove from heat. Cover and set aside to cool for about 15 minutes.

2. For the roll dough: In the bowl of an electric mixer fitted with the dough hook, combine flour, salt, yeast, and dry milk. Add warm milk, eggs, melted butter,

Continued on next page

and warm tangzhong paste. Mix on medium speed until just combined, 1 to 2 minutes. Dough will be sticky and rough. Cover bowl with a clean towel or lid and let rest 20 minutes.

3. After 20 minutes, mix dough on medium-high speed until a smooth dough forms, about 2 minutes.

4. Remove dough hook and scrape down sides of bowl. Loosely form dough into a ball in the bottom of the bowl (or transfer dough to a separate greased bowl). Cover and transfer to a warm place to proof. Let rise until almost doubled in bulk and a finger imprint remains and doesn't bounce back when touched, 60 to 80 minutes.

5. For the filling: In a medium saucepan, whisk together sugar, salt, egg yolks, and half the coconut milk until a smooth mixture forms. Whisk in the remaining coconut milk and add butter, then place the pan over medium-high heat. Stir constantly until mixture comes to a boil. Reduce heat to a full simmer and let cook until thickened, stirring occasionally, about 12 minutes total. Add coconut extract and shredded coconut, then set aside. Mixture will thicken more as it cools.

6. When dough has proofed, turn it out onto a floured work surface. Gently press into a rectangle shape, then roll into a 12-by-19-inch rectangle.

7. Spread cooled filling over the entire surface. Starting on the long edge, roll dough into a log, like cinnamon rolls. Turn the log so the open edge is on the bottom to secure it. The length of the log may have expanded, or you can gently stretch it to be about 22 inches.

8. Use a thread or knife to cut the log into 15 or 16 rolls. Place rolls cut side up in a greased or parchment-lined jelly roll pan (10-by-15-inch pan) or in smaller pans as desired, about ½ to 1 inch apart.

9. Cover pan(s) and let rolls rise until almost doubled in bulk, 45 to 60 minutes.

10. When rolls are almost proofed completely, heat oven to 350°F with rack in the center. Bake rolls until just turning golden but still blonde in parts, 22 to 26 minutes. Do not undercook. Let cool for a bit.

11. For the buttercream: Blend together butter, cream cheese, salt, and coconut extract until smooth. Add confectioners' sugar a bit at a time until frosting is smooth and fluffy. Spread icing on warm or cooled rolls. Sprinkle with extra toasted coconut if desired. Rolls can be kept at room temperature covered with plastic wrap up to 2 days. Reheat in the microwave for a few seconds if desired.

NOTE If you are filling two smaller pans with rolls, you can immediately wrap and freeze one pan for up to a month. To bake, remove from the freezer and let rise overnight in the fridge or about 4 hours on the counter, then bake as directed.

MAKES

1 STANDARD LOAF
OR 3 MINI LOAVES

HANDS-ON TIME

30 MINUTES

TOTAL TIME

1 HOUR 30 MINUTES

TARA'S TIP

Adding 2 tablespoons poppy seeds with the flour is a classic twist and highly recommended if you're willing to veer from unadulterated perfection.

perfect lemon loaf cake

I LOVE INDULGING in a soft, tender slice of lemon cake at the bakeries and coffee shops in New York. The best is when there's a super lemony icing on top.

Recreating my vision of the perfect lemon loaf cake proved harder than I thought it would be. It went through many, many tests before landing on the final result. I wanted a tender, fine crumb for the cake. I wanted it to be soft and tasty but not oily or overly buttery. I didn't want it to be too sweet because the glaze, while tangy, is very sweet.

Instead of adding more lemon juice (extra liquid would just make the cake crumb coarse and chewy), I reduced fresh lemon juice on the stove to create an ultra-concentrated syrup. Just 2 tablespoons of the stuff worked wonders. Paired with loads of lemon zest in the batter and a splash of lemon extract for that bakery taste, the cake itself is gloriously citrusy. Making this in mini loaf pans is great for brunches or gifting.

LEMON LOAF CAKE

⅓ cup fresh lemon juice	¾ teaspoon fine salt
½ cup sour cream	1 teaspoon baking powder
1½ tablespoons lemon zest	¼ teaspoon baking soda
2 teaspoons lemon extract	½ cup unsalted butter, softened
½ teaspoon vanilla extract	1 cup granulated sugar
1½ cups (192 g) all-purpose flour	3 large eggs, room temperature

LEMON ICING

1 cup confectioners' sugar	4 teaspoons fresh lemon juice

1. For the cake: Heat oven to 350°F. In a small saucepan over medium-high heat, bring lemon juice to a boil. Boil until juice is reduced to 2 tablespoons, 3 to 5 minutes. Remove from heat and use a rubber spatula to get all the reduced juice out of the pan and into a small bowl. Stir in sour cream, lemon zest, lemon extract, and vanilla extract. Set aside.

2. Spray a standard loaf pan (8½-by-4½-inch) or three 3-by-5½-inch mini loaf pans with cooking spray and line with a piece of parchment that overhangs on two sides (see page 221 for example). Set pan(s) aside.

3. In a bowl, whisk together flour, salt, baking powder, and baking soda. Set aside.

4. In the bowl of an electric mixer fitted with the paddle attachment, beat butter and sugar together until pale and fluffy, about 2 minutes. Add eggs one at a time, beating well and scraping down sides of bowl after each egg is added.

5. Add half the flour mixture and mix until just combined. Then add sour cream mixture and blend. Finally, add remaining flour. Beat to combine but don't overmix.

6. Spoon batter into prepared pan(s). (If making minis, you should have 1½ cups batter for each small pan.) If using one standard loaf pan, bake 50 to 55 minutes

Continued on next page

or until a cake tester inserted into center of cake comes out clean. If using three mini loaf pans, bake 25 to 30 minutes or until a cake tester inserted into center of cakes comes out clean.

7. Remove from oven and cool in pan on a wire rack 10 minutes. Run a knife around the edge, then, using the parchment, carefully lift cake from pan. Let cool completely on wire rack.

8. For the lemon icing: Once the cake is cool, in a small bowl, use a wooden or metal spoon to stir together confectioners' sugar and lemon juice. Mixture will be very thick. Spoon glaze over the top of the cake and gently spread evenly, almost to the edges, allowing some to drizzle down the sides. Let glaze set 20 to 30 minutes before serving. Store cake wrapped, in a cool place, up to 3 days.

blueberry bannock scone

MAKES

8 SERVINGS,
1 (9-INCH) SCONE

HANDS-ON TIME

30 MINUTES

TOTAL TIME

1 HOUR

TRADITIONAL SCOTTISH bannock cakes are baked on a griddle, but I make a simple one in the oven to serve the whole family. I've added wheat germ instead of whole wheat flour to give the quick bread a nutty but light texture, and finely chopped pecans add amazing flavor.

I've stuffed my bannock with blueberries, which takes an extra step to get them nestled in a layer, but it's well worth it when you slice into a molten-berry middle! My biggest tip is to use a gentle hand and not overwork the dough.

SCONE

- 1¼ cups (160 g) all-purpose flour, plus more for baking sheet
- ½ cup finely chopped pecans
- ½ cup wheat germ
- 1 tablespoon baking powder
- ½ teaspoon fine salt
- ½ teaspoon cinnamon
- 5 tablespoons granulated sugar, divided
- ⅓ cup unsalted butter, cut up and chilled
- ½ cup buttermilk
- 2 large eggs, divided
- 1¼ cups fresh blueberries
- 1 teaspoon water

ICING

- ¾ cup confectioners' sugar
- 2 to 3 tablespoons milk

1. For the scone: Heat oven to 400°F. Use the top of a bowl to draw an 8- or 9-inch circle on a piece of parchment paper as a guide. Set aside on a baking sheet.

2. In a large bowl, combine flour, pecans, wheat germ, baking powder, salt, cinnamon, and 4 tablespoons sugar. Use a pastry blender to cut butter into flour mixture until mixture forms small crumbs with tiny bits of butter.

3. In another bowl, combine buttermilk and 1 egg. Add to flour mixture and stir until just moistened. Dough will seem wet and sticky, but work it as little as possible.

4. Divide dough in half and use two spoons to dollop half the dough around the circle marked on the prepared baking sheet. With floured hands, shape the dollops into one

Spoon batter over blueberries, then gently press together to form the top of the scone, sealing the edges around the blueberries.

Continued on next page

circle. Spread blueberries evenly over the scone, leaving a ½-inch border. Sprinkle with remaining 1 tablespoon sugar.

5. Using spoons again, dollop remaining dough over blueberries, then with floured hands press together to make a top layer, covering the berries.

6. Beat remaining egg with water and brush some on top of the scone. Score into 8 wedges on top. Bake until scone is golden brown, 20 to 25 minutes.

7. For the icing: Stir together confectioners' sugar and milk to make a thick icing. When scone is almost cool, drizzle with icing.

MAKES

12 MUFFINS

HANDS-ON TIME

20 MINUTES

TOTAL TIME

35 MINUTES

cheesecake-topped whole-wheat brown sugar muffins

MY FAMILY MOST OFTEN eats muffins alongside dinner, even Sunday dinner! I kind of love that we take a typical breakfast food and give it a place at the end of the day. I grew up with this recipe for brown sugar muffins from my Aunt Kayln, and if you dare stray from breakfast, serve them for dinner with my Pot Roast (page 61) like Mom used to (so good!).

I've made a humble whole wheat quick bread even better by adding a cheesecake topping. It acts almost like a luscious frosting on these over-the-top-amazing breakfast, brunch, or dinner muffins.

CHEESECAKE TOPPING

4 ounces cream cheese, softened

1 large egg yolk

¼ cup granulated sugar

BROWN SUGAR MUFFINS

2 cups (260 g) whole wheat flour

½ teaspoon fine salt

1 teaspoon baking soda

½ cup (1 stick) unsalted butter, softened

1 cup packed light brown sugar

1 large egg

1 teaspoon vanilla extract

1 cup milk

1 cup (4 ounces) chopped pecans, divided

1. Heat oven to 425°F. Line a standard muffin pan with paper cups. Set aside.

2. For the topping: In a medium bowl with an electric mixer, blend all topping ingredients. Set aside.

3. For the muffins: In a bowl, whisk together whole wheat flour, salt, and baking soda. Set aside.

4. In a bowl with an electric mixer (you may use the same beaters as for the topping ingredients), cream together butter and brown sugar until just lightened, about 2 minutes. Mix in egg and vanilla. Add flour mixture and milk alternately in two batches, mixing between each addition. Stir in ¾ cup nuts.

5. Divide batter between muffin cups (each will get about ⅓ cup batter). Spoon a generous tablespoon cream-cheese mixture onto the center of each muffin, then sprinkle all muffins with remaining ¼ cup chopped nuts.

6. Bake muffins until cooked through, 12 to 14 minutes. Remove and let cool a few minutes or completely before serving.

BAKING
AND SWEETS

This chapter makes me so happy! I have such a sweet tooth and tend to bake a lot. Baking is something I do for fun. It's relaxing, and there's always a guaranteed sugary bonus at the end!

I get such joy from sharing food with people, and there's nothing better than listening to the "mmms" and "ahhs" as everyone eats the cake or warm chocolate chip cookies I just made. Every dessert in this chapter met with such adoration when I shared the first iterations with family and friends that not one could be left out!

There are some sentimental family favorites passed down from my mom, of course, like a delicious chocolate cake, a fresh peach pie with sweet cream cheese, and my favorite apple pudding cake with butter sauce. But you'll also find irresistible things I conjured up from sketches and my imagination, like passion fruit meringue tart with a coconut cookie crust and a peanut butter ice cream dessert.

Whatever you try, I hope you find joy in sharing these recipes too.

blackberry and lemon curd swirled ice cream

MAKES

2½ PINTS

HANDS-ON TIME

45 MINUTES

TOTAL TIME

8 HOURS
45 MINUTES

I LOVE A FANCY SCHMANCY ice cream, but I also love a shortcut. You can spruce up store-bought vanilla ice cream with all sorts of amazing swirls and bits rather than make and churn your own. If you like everything from scratch, then by all means follow the recipes on TaraTeaspoon.com for homemade ice cream. Otherwise, use my cheater's version to create complete bliss! Work quickly to swirl your additions into softened ice cream, then refreeze and you're done. Double the recipe and keep some in the freezer for later too!

The swirls are the most important part of this frozen delight, so prep a day ahead and have them ready in the fridge. Fresh lemon curd is divine, but you can also use store-bought, and the mix of blackberries with lemon will be your new favorite combo!

Scooped onto a cone or bowl, over a slice of cake, or with some shortbread cookies, this treat is magical, to say the least.

LEMON CURD SWIRL

½ cup (1 stick) unsalted butter

3 tablespoons lemon zest from 2 to 3 lemons

½ cup fresh lemon juice

⅛ teaspoon fine salt

¾ cup granulated sugar

6 large egg yolks

BLACKBERRY SWIRL

2 tablespoons water

1¼ teaspoons unflavored gelatin

1¼ cups (6 ounces) blackberries

⅓ cup granulated sugar

2 teaspoons fresh lemon juice

ICE CREAM

2 pints vanilla ice cream

> **TARA'S TIP**
>
> Short on time? You can chill the lemon curd and blackberry swirls over an ice bath instead of in the fridge. Fill large bowls with ice and a little water. Place the bowls of filling on top of the ice and water. Stir fillings occasionally until mixtures cool and thicken. Then store in the fridge until ready to use.

1. For the lemon curd swirl: Melt butter in a medium saucepan over medium-high heat. Once butter is melted, add lemon zest, lemon juice, salt, and sugar. Whisk to combine. Whisk in egg yolks until smooth.

2. Reduce heat to medium-low and cook, whisking constantly, until mixture thickens, 5 to 8 minutes. Don't let the mixture boil. (You can use this classic trick to check if the mixture is thick enough: Dip a wooden spoon into the curd and draw your finger across the spoon. Your finger should leave a path, and the curd won't run to fill it in.) Once thickened, immediately pour through a fine-mesh sieve into a bowl. Use a rubber spatula to force all the curd through the sieve, leaving just the zest and any cooked bits of egg in the sieve. Dispose of zest and leftover egg. Scrape the bottom of the sieve to retrieve all the curd. Cover and refrigerate until thick, about 4 hours. Curd will keep in the fridge up to 2 weeks.

Continued on next page

3. For the blackberry swirl: Place water in a small bowl and sprinkle gelatin over the top. Let it soften (bloom) in the water.

4. Pulse blackberries in a food processor or mash them in a medium saucepan until juicy but not puréed. Add bloomed gelatin, sugar, and lemon juice. Bring to a simmer over medium heat, then remove from heat. Stir until sugar and gelatin are dissolved. Cool and refrigerate until ready to use.

5. For the ice cream: Stir chilled lemon curd until soft and smooth. Then, working quickly, scoop ice cream into the bowl of an electric mixer fitted with the paddle attachment. Add half the lemon curd and mix just until ice cream is softened. (It will look like a really thick milkshake.) Working quickly, spoon some lemon ice cream into an ice-cream container or large loaf pan. Spoon some lemon curd swirl and blackberry swirl on top. Repeat layering with ice cream and fillings until they are used up. Cover and freeze at least 4 hours or overnight before serving.

coconut bundt cake

REAL HEROES don't wear capes . . . They wear a perfect drizzle of frosting and a sprinkle of coconut! This cake is my dessert hero, and you'll know why once you taste it. I blend some of the coconut into the cake batter and use coconut milk to create a rich, decadent texture and flavor. This cake is easy enough to make for any regular meal but impressive enough to serve at a party, shower, or Easter dinner. Try serving it with fresh raspberries for a real thrill.

SERVES

8 TO 10

MAKES

1 (8-INCH) BUNDT CAKE

HANDS-ON TIME

30 MINUTES

TOTAL TIME

2 HOURS 20 MINUTES

CAKE

¾ cup (3 ounces) sweetened shredded coconut

1¾ cups (224 g) all-purpose flour, plus more for pan

2 teaspoons baking powder

½ teaspoon fine salt

¾ cup (1½ sticks) unsalted butter, softened, plus more for pan

1⅓ cups granulated sugar

2 large eggs

2 large egg whites

1½ teaspoons vanilla extract

¾ cup canned unsweetened coconut milk

ICING

1½ cups confectioners' sugar

3 tablespoons canned unsweetened coconut milk

½ cup (2 ounces) sweetened shredded coconut, for topping

> **TARA'S TIP**
>
> Make 12 cupcakes instead of a cake. Fill cupcake papers with a generous ⅓ cup batter and bake until tops spring back when touched, 15 to 17 minutes.

1. Heat oven to 350°F. Generously butter and flour an 8-inch (6-cup capacity) Bundt pan. Set aside.

2. In a food processor, pulse shredded coconut, flour, baking powder, and salt until combined and until coconut is very finely chopped.

3. In a mixing bowl, beat butter until creamy. Gradually add sugar on medium-high speed until mixture is light and fluffy, 2 to 3 minutes. Add eggs, egg whites, and vanilla. Beat until incorporated.

4. Add flour mixture to the batter in three parts, alternately with the coconut milk, starting and ending with flour, stirring between each addition. Scrape down sides of bowl occasionally.

5. Pour batter into prepared pan. Bake until a cake tester inserted into the middle of the cake comes out clean, 35 to 37 minutes. Transfer to a wire rack and let cool in pan for 30 minutes.

6. Trim top of cake with a serrated knife to make a flat base for when you flip it over, if desired. Run a small knife around the edge to loosen, then invert cake onto a rack to cool completely.

7. For the icing: Whisk confectioners' sugar and coconut milk into a thick icing. Drizzle icing over cake and top with shredded coconut.

NOTE This cake is not a standard size Bundt. Use an 8-inch Bundt pan to re-create the picture.

SERVES

9

TOTAL TIME

35 MINUTES,
NOT INCLUDING
CORNBREAD
PREPARATION

TARA'S TIP

You'll have great
success making this
year-round. In the
summer, use fresh
fruit. The rest of
the year, use frozen
blackberries and
peaches. Just thaw
and drain the peaches
before tossing with
sugar. The frozen
blackberries can
be used directly
in the sauce.

blackberry and peach cornbread shortcake

PEACHES AND BLACKBERRIES are late-summer stars and are actually a pretty classic combination in crisps, pies, and summer desserts. I happen to love the pairing of sweet corn and blackberries and couldn't resist using my Golden Sweet Cornbread (page 88) as the cake base for this traditional treat. The cornbread is soft and sweet and proudly holds the juicy peaches, blackberries, and clouds of whipped cream. You'll be surprised by how much you love it! This is a great dessert for Sunday dinner or a backyard BBQ, and it's a delicious way to use any leftover cornbread from the day before.

SHORTCAKE

1 recipe Golden Sweet Cornbread
(page 88), prepared and then
baked according to step 1 below

BLACKBERRY SAUCE

2½ cups (12 ounces) blackberries

2 tablespoons fresh lemon juice

½ cup granulated sugar

2 teaspoons cornstarch

¾ cup water

TOPPING

3 cups sliced peaches from 5 or 6
small peaches

2 teaspoons granulated sugar

1 cup heavy cream

⅓ cup confectioners' sugar

1 teaspoon vanilla extract

1¼ cups (6 ounces) blackberries

1. For the cornbread: Prepare the cornbread recipe but bake it in a 9-inch round cake pan. The baking time will be 30 to 35 minutes.
2. For the blackberry sauce: In a medium saucepan over medium-high heat, combine all blackberry sauce ingredients. Use a potato masher or spoon to crush the berries into a sauce as they cook. Once sauce comes to a boil, reduce heat and simmer about 1 minute. Remove from heat and let cool.
3. For topping: Toss peaches with granulated sugar and set aside.
4. With an electric mixer, whip cream, confectioners' sugar, and vanilla until the cream holds soft peaks. Set aside.
5. Cut cornbread into wedges and slice in half horizontally. On individual plates, cover the bottom half of each wedge with some peaches, fresh blackberries, cream, and blackberry sauce. Cover with cornbread tops and add a little more cream, fresh blackberries, and extra blackberry sauce to serve.

apple pudding cake with butter sauce

SERVES

12 TO 14

HANDS-ON TIME

40 MINUTES

TOTAL TIME

2 HOURS
55 MINUTES

HANDS DOWN, this is my all-time favorite dessert. Wait! Did I just say that out loud? If the other treats and desserts didn't hear that, just keep it between us. I love all things dessert and usually don't pick favorites, but this one can claim the top of the list.

This rich cake, reminiscent of the dense steamed puddings my grandma used to make, is our family Christmas dessert—although we've been known to make it year-round, especially during peak apple season in the fall. It's subtly spiced and full of the tart and sweet taste of apples, plus crunchy pecans. To make the cake even more special for the holidays, top with Apple Crisps (page 214).

You may think adding the sauce is gilding the lily, as the cake on its own is delicious. But in my opinion, the sauce is essential and makes each bite of cake extra divine.

APPLE PUDDING CAKE

2 cups (256 g) all-purpose flour

1 cup (4½ ounces) chopped pecans

½ teaspoon nutmeg

2 teaspoons ground cinnamon

2 teaspoons baking soda

1 teaspoon fine salt

4 cups grated apple, any variety, from 3 to 4 cored apples

½ cup unsalted butter, softened, plus more for pan

2 cups granulated sugar, plus more for pan

2 large eggs

BUTTER SAUCE

¾ cup (1½ sticks) unsalted butter

3 cups granulated sugar

1½ cups (12-ounce can) evaporated milk

4 teaspoons vanilla extract

⅛ teaspoon nutmeg

> **TARA'S TIP**
> I make this cake in a fun tube pan for the wow factor at the holidays, but it bakes perfectly in a 9-by-13-inch cake pan. Bake about 35 minutes.

1. For the cake: Heat oven to 350°F. Brush a 10- or 12-cup Bundt pan generously with extra butter. Sprinkle pan with extra sugar, then tap out excess. Set pan aside.

2. Stir together flour, pecans, nutmeg, cinnamon, baking soda, and salt. Set aside.

3. In a food processor or with a box grater, shred apples with the skin on. You should have 4 cups grated apple.

4. In a mixer, cream together butter and sugar with the paddle attachment. Add eggs and beat until mixture is fluffy. Stir in apples (and any juice they produce) and flour mixture until completely combined. Spoon batter into prepared pan and smooth top.

5. Bake until a cake tester inserted into the center of the cake comes out clean and cake pulls slightly away from the sides of the pan, about 1 hour 10 minutes. Tent cake with foil for the last half hour of baking to prevent overbrowning.

Continued on next page

6. Let cool on a wire rack, about 20 minutes, then invert onto a cooling rack to remove from pan. Let cool completely.

7. For the butter sauce: In a saucepan over medium-low heat, simmer all butter sauce ingredients, stirring, for 12 minutes. Remove from heat and cool slightly. Sauce will thicken as it cools. Serve the sauce warm over slices of cake, or serve sauce on the side and let guests add a generous amount of warm sauce to each slice of cake.

8. Garnish with apple crisps, if desired.

NOTE The cake and sauce can be made a day in advance. Allow both to cool completely before storing. Cover cake with plastic wrap and store at room temperature. Refrigerate butter sauce and reheat in microwave or saucepan to serve.

apple crisps

2 apples   **Confectioners' sugar, for dusting**

1. Heat oven to 250°F. Thinly slice apples using a mandoline. Place on a baking sheet lined with parchment or a silpat liner.

2. Use a sieve to lightly dust both sides of each slice with confectioners' sugar.

3. Bake one to two hours, turning apples over once during baking. To test doneness, remove one slice and let it cool. It will be crispy when cooled, and the apples will be done.

4. Remove from oven and quickly transfer apples to a wire rack and let cool.

secret chocolate cake

SERVES

15

MAKES

1 (11-BY-15-INCH)
CAKE, OR 28
CUPCAKES

HANDS-ON TIME

30 MINUTES

TOTAL TIME

1 HOUR 50 MINUTES

YOU'RE NOT SUPPOSED to have this chocolate cake recipe . . .

Originally served at the now-closed Keeley's Cafe in Salt Lake City, Utah, it was passed down to Grandma Keeley's daughter Jolene, who made it for neighbors. One of those neighbors was my mother, who asked her dear friend Jolene for the recipe. And there it began.

Mom was given the recipe as long as she promised to keep it to herself. But she received the recipe for only the cake! Mom said, "But what about the frosting?" Jolene said, "I didn't give it to you—that's the best part!" and wouldn't hand it over. With time and persuasion, this recipe—*with* the frosting—was eventually passed to Mom, who eventually passed to me, and I'm sharing it with you! (I didn't make any secret promises, after all.)

To add flavor, I took liberties and swapped the original shortening in the cake for butter. However, the shortening called for in the frosting, in my opinion, isn't optional. Now shortening is my mom's secret weapon for an ultra silky-smooth frosting. The frosting is the reason she wanted the recipe in the first place! That little bit of shortening makes a difference.

The cake is feathery light with a fine crumb. It can be made into a sheet cake, baked in 9-inch round pans, or made into cupcakes. It's a generous recipe, but that means it's perfect to share—as it always should have been!

SECRET CHOCOLATE CAKE

3 ounces unsweetened chocolate, chopped

2 teaspoons baking soda

1 cup boiling water

1 cup (2 sticks) unsalted butter, softened

2 cups granulated sugar

1 teaspoon fine salt

1 tablespoon vanilla extract

4 large eggs, room temperature

3 cups (390 g) cake flour

1 cup buttermilk

SILKY MILK CHOCOLATE FROSTING

½ cup (1 stick) unsalted butter, softened

2 tablespoons vegetable shortening

½ cup plus 2 tablespoons unsweetened cocoa powder

4 cups confectioners' sugar (sifted if lumpy)

1 teaspoon vanilla extract

½ to ¾ cup milk

> **TARA'S TIP**
>
> An 11-by-15-inch cake pan is bigger than your classic 9-by-13-inch. If you don't have one, use about 6½ cups cake batter in a 9-by-13-inch pan and use the rest of the batter for cupcakes.

1. For the cake: Heat oven to 350°F. Butter an 11-by-15-inch cake pan. Set aside.

2. In a large saucepan over medium heat, melt unsweetened chocolate, whisking constantly. Once melted, add baking soda and boiling water. Whisk well, then remove from heat. Mixture will bubble a lot.

3. In an electric mixer fitted with the paddle attachment, cream together butter,

Continued on next page

BAKING AND SWEETS

sugar, and salt on medium-high speed until light and fluffy, 1 to 2 minutes. Add vanilla. Then add eggs one at a time, beating to combine after each.

4. Add flour to the batter in three parts alternately with the milk, starting and ending with flour, stirring between each addition. Scrape down the bowl as necessary. Then add melted chocolate mixture and gently stir until combined. Batter will be liquidy.

5. Transfer batter to prepared pan. Bake until the center of the cake springs back when lightly touched, 30 to 35 minutes. Cool before frosting.

6. For the frosting: In the clean bowl of a mixer with the paddle attachment, cream butter, shortening, and cocoa until smooth. Add confectioners' sugar a little at a time. Add vanilla extract and ½ cup milk and mix until smooth and creamy. Add more milk, a little at a time, to get the consistency you like. Frost cake.

VARIATIONS

CUPCAKES: Make 28 cupcakes from a full batch or 14 cupcakes from half a recipe. Fill cupcake papers with ¼ cup batter and bake until tops spring back when touched, 18 to 20 minutes.

ROUND CAKES: Grease and line 2 (9-by-2-inch round) cake pans with parchment. Bake cakes about 30 minutes.

chilled strawberries-and-cream soufflé

THE KID IN ME comes out when I make this strawberries-and-cream dessert—I lick every beater and spoon available at the end of cooking. It's irresistible!

With just a few simple ingredients, you can whip up this luscious pink mousse loaded with tangy-sweet strawberries and silky cream. The mousse is chilled on top of a cookie crust and garnished with crunchy bits of freeze-dried strawberries. It's the perfect dessert for spring and summer when you're craving a burst of fresh berries. Or you can use frozen strawberries to make it any time of the year, like for Valentine's!

As a variation, you can skip the crust and chill the mousse in individual bowls for a special party treat.

COOKIE CRUST

40 vanilla wafer cookies

2 tablespoons granulated sugar

4 tablespoons (½ stick) unsalted butter, melted

MOUSSE

6 cups strawberry puree from 4 pints (3 pounds) strawberries, rinsed and hulled (thawed if frozen)

¼ cup fresh lemon juice

3 cups granulated sugar

6 teaspoons unflavored gelatin

¼ cup cold water

2 cups heavy cream, divided

TOPPING

2 tablespoons granulated sugar

1 cup heavy cream

Freeze-dried strawberries, crushed, for garnish

1. For the cookie crust: Heat oven to 350°F. Cover the bottom of a 9-inch springform pan with a circle of parchment and set aside.

2. In a food processor, combine cookies and sugar. Blend until cookies are finely crushed. Add butter and blend until completely combined.

3. Press crust crumbs onto the bottom of prepared pan. Crust will be just under ¼-inch thick. Bake 7 minutes, then set aside to cool.

4. For the mousse: In a blender or food processor, purée strawberries, lemon juice, and sugar. Press mixture through a fine sieve into a bowl, discarding pulp. You should have 6 cups purée. If there is excess, save for another use.

5. Prepare an ice bath by filling a large bowl with ice and a little water. Set aside.

6. In a medium heatproof bowl set over a pan of simmering water, dissolve gelatin in cold water. Add 1½ cups strawberry purée and stir to combine with gelatin. Return strawberry-gelatin mixture to the bowl with remaining strawberry

Continued on next page

purée and stir to combine. (If you'd like to make swirls on top, set aside ½ cup purée mixture now and keep at room temperature.)

7. Set the bowl of strawberry-gelatin purée over the ice bath. Stir frequently until mixture is chilled and slightly thick, about 20 minutes.

8. In a separate bowl, whip cream to stiff peaks. Fold into chilled strawberry purée.

9. Transfer mousse to pan with crust. (If making swirls, spoon reserved purée on top in 1-inch dots and drag a skewer through the center of each to make a swirled heart.) Transfer dessert to the fridge and chill until set, at least 4 hours and up to 8 hours.

10. To serve, run a knife around the edges to loosen. Remove the springform ring and transfer dessert to a serving platter, removing parchment.

11. For the topping: Whip sugar and cream to soft peaks and spoon on top. Garnish with crushed freeze-dried strawberries.

For a fun variation on the strawberry soufflé: The strawberry mousse filling makes about five ½ cups. To make sweet little desserts for a party, skip the crust and portion the filling into individual serving dishes, then chill until set.

LINING PANS

Lining baking pans with parchment is insurance for a perfect finished product. For round pans, trace the pan on the paper and cut just inside the line so the parchment circle fits inside and doesn't crinkle up the edges. For loaf pans, use one or two strips of parchment that fit inside the smallest edges near the bottom of the pan. Leave extra overhang to help you lift the loaf out. Do the same thing for square or rectangular pans. If the overhang flops around, use a metal binder clip (it's ovenproof!) to hold the paper down. Once cool, you can remove the clips and lift your dessert out of the pan.

sunken chocolate cakes with hot fudge sauce

THESE INDIVIDUAL DESSERTS are the unfussy sisters to the much-beloved flourless chocolate cake. I think a fudgy, ultra-chocolatey cake is great, but what if you got your own mini version—and what if that little mini version sank perfectly to hold your scoop of ice cream and hot fudge? It's amazing—that's what it is! Genius for a casual gathering.

Coat muffin tins with butter and sugar to give these little cakes a sweet, crunchy outside. Fill them with a scoop of vanilla or your favorite ice cream, and drool—I mean *drizzle* on the hot fudge.

SERVES

8

HANDS-ON TIME

40 MINUTES

TOTAL TIME

1 HOUR

CAKE

- ½ cup (1 stick) butter, cut into pieces, plus more for pan
- 5 ounces bittersweet chocolate, chopped
- 4 tablespoons granulated sugar, divided, plus extra for pan
- 2 large eggs, separated
- 2 large egg yolks
- ¼ teaspoon fine salt
- 1 teaspoon vanilla extract
- Ice cream

HOT FUDGE SAUCE

- 2 cups granulated sugar
- ¼ cup unsweetened cocoa powder
- ½ cup (1 stick) unsalted butter
- ¾ cup evaporated milk
- ½ teaspoon vanilla extract
- Pinch salt

1. Heat oven to 350°F. Brush 8 cups of a standard muffin tin with extra softened butter. Coat with extra sugar, then tap out excess. Set aside.

2. In a bowl in the microwave or saucepan on the stove, melt together butter and chocolate. Set aside and let cool slightly.

3. In a mixing bowl, combine 4 egg yolks with 2 tablespoons sugar. Whip until mixture is pale yellow and thick, 4 to 5 minutes. Stir in salt, vanilla extract, and melted chocolate mixture.

4. In a separate bowl, beat egg whites until soft peaks form. Add remaining 2 tablespoons sugar. Whisk until stiff and shiny but not dry. Fold egg white mixture into chocolate mixture.

5. Divide batter evenly among prepared muffin cups. Bake until set and slightly springy to the touch, 10 to 12 minutes. Do not overbake; they will still be a bit shiny in parts.

6. Remove muffin pan from oven and transfer to a wire rack. Cool for 15 minutes in pan, then carefully run a knife around the edges of each cake and unmold.

7. To make hot fudge sauce: In a saucepan, whisk together sugar and cocoa. Add butter and milk. Heat over medium-high heat, stirring. Once butter has melted, cook 5 minutes more, stirring constantly. Remove from heat. Add vanilla and salt.

8. Serve cake warm with ice cream and hot fudge sauce.

TARA'S TIP

These cakes are best served warm, so I suggest measuring and prepping all the ingredients beforehand. (You can even melt the butter and chocolate together ahead of time.) Then assemble and bake just before you want to serve them. It won't take long!

Hot Fudge Sauce can be made in advance, cooled, and stored in the fridge for up to a week. Reheat on the stove or in the microwave to serve.

MAKES

6 TO 8 SERVINGS,
1 (9-INCH) PIE

HANDS-ON TIME

50 MINUTES, NOT
INCLUDING CRUST
PREPARATION

TOTAL TIME

6 HOURS

TARA'S TIP

The glaze makes enough for two pies. Save leftover glaze in the fridge for up to a week for another pie! Melt it in the microwave about 20 seconds and whisk until smooth before using.

fresh peach pie with sweet cream cheese

THE SECOND Lemon Elberta peaches are in season, this pie is on repeat at our house. For only a few short weeks, it's almost a daily occurrence. No one complains. You see, this pie is special: it's the best pie in the world. You don't believe me? Try it!

What's great is that while Lemon Elbertas are pure gold as far as peaches go, this pie is divine with any fresh peach and even frozen peaches! The hidden layer of sweetened cream cheese makes an appearance with each bite and creates the luxurious taste of peaches and cream. Delish!

PIE CRUST

1 crust from Classic Pie Crust (page 227), blind-baked and set aside to cool

GLAZE

3 tablespoons orange Jell-O powder (from a box of orange Jell-O)

¼ cup very hot water

½ cup cold water

3 tablespoons cornstarch

1 tablespoon fresh lemon juice

¼ cup granulated sugar

CREAM CHEESE LAYER

4 ounces cream cheese, room temperature

½ cup confectioners' sugar

½ teaspoon vanilla extract

PEACH PIE

5 cups sliced freestone peaches from 5 to 6 peaches

1 teaspoon vanilla extract

1¼ cups heavy cream

⅓ cup confectioners' sugar

1. For the glaze: Dissolve orange Jell-O in very hot water. Set aside.
2. In a small saucepan, whisk together cold water, cornstarch, lemon juice, and sugar. Stir over medium heat until boiling, then simmer 30 seconds (mixture will be thick). Remove from heat. Add orange Jell-O and stir to combine. Cover and let cool. (You can also set the glaze over an ice bath, stirring occasionally, to cool faster.)
3. For the cream cheese layer: With an electric mixer, beat all cream cheese layer ingredients until very smooth. Spread mixture in the baked and cooled pie crust along the bottom and about 1 inch up the sides.
4. For the peach pie: Peel peaches, remove pits, and slice into ¼-inch slices. You should have about 5 cups sliced peaches.

Continued on next page

5. In a large bowl, gently stir peaches with ½ cup glaze to coat evenly. Set aside remaining glaze (see Tara's Tip). Transfer glazed peaches to pie crust, scraping all the glaze out of the bowl into the crust. Cover with plastic wrap and chill 4 to 6 hours.

6. When ready to serve, combine vanilla, heavy cream, and confectioners' sugar in a large mixing bowl and whip until soft peaks form. Dollop on the pie and slice to serve.

NOTE If using frozen peaches, let them thaw on a cooling rack set over a baking sheet to catch all the juices. You can use any of the juices as part of the ½ cup cold water in the glaze if you'd like.

classic pie crust

MY GO-TO pie crust recipe has butter and shortening for the best of both worlds. The butter gives it amazing flavor and crispness, and the shortening makes lovely tender flakes. The addition of vinegar both tenderizes and adds a subtle acidity for flavor.

MAKES

2 SINGLE CRUSTS

HANDS-ON TIME

20 MINUTES

TOTAL TIME

45 MINUTES

½ cup very cold water

1 tablespoon white vinegar

2½ cups (320 g) all-purpose flour

1 teaspoon fine salt

1 teaspoon granulated sugar

¾ cup (1½ sticks) unsalted butter, cold, cut into pieces

¼ cup shortening, chilled

1. Mix together water and vinegar and set aside.
2. In a food processor, mix flour, salt, and sugar. Add butter and shortening and pulse until butter is the size of peas.
3. Add ⅓ cup water-vinegar mixture in a slow stream and pulse several times. Pinch dough to see if it is holding together. If it's not, add more water-vinegar mixture, 1 tablespoon at a time, pulsing once or twice after each addition, until dough just holds together. You may dispose of any leftover water-vinegar mixture.
4. Gather dough together and divide in half. Form dough into two disks. Wrap each disk in plastic wrap and chill 30 minutes before using. Dough disks can be chilled up to a week or frozen up to a month.

BLIND-BAKED SINGLE CRUST

1. Heat oven to 375°F. On a floured work surface, roll one crust into a circle about 12 inches in diameter. Gently fit into a 9-inch pie pan. Trim edge so it hangs ½ inch over the lip of the pie pan. Tuck overhang under to create a clean edge and crimp as desired. Freeze crust for 20 minutes.
2. Line frozen crust with a circle of parchment larger than the pie and fill with baking beans or baking weights. Bake until edges begin to brown, 12 to 15 minutes. Carefully remove parchment with beans and bake until the center of the crust turns light golden brown, an additional 10 to 12 minutes. Let cool before filling.

This is my favorite place to be in the kitchen, right next to my mom, Mary, cooking together.

browned-butter toffee blondies

UNTIL THIS RECIPE, blondies didn't do a whole lot for me. They just didn't have enough chocolate! (Wink!) Blondies aren't brownies, but they are brownies' delicious relative. These cookie bars have the same texture and buttery richness without the chocolate.

This cookie bar is great for a party dessert platter, and the browned-butter flavor paired with toffee bits knocks everyone's socks off! I encourage creativity with this recipe: swap the walnuts for hazelnuts, macadamias, or another favorite nut for a unique treat.

MAKES

16 SERVINGS,
1 (9-BY-13-INCH)
PAN

HANDS-ON TIME

30 MINUTES

TOTAL TIME

1 HOUR 20 MINUTES

1¼ cups (2½ sticks) unsalted butter	½ cup granulated sugar
2¼ cups (288 g) all-purpose flour	3 large eggs
1½ teaspoons baking powder	2½ teaspoons vanilla extract
1½ teaspoons fine salt	1 cup (4 ounces) chopped walnuts
2 cups packed light brown sugar	1 cup toffee bits

1. Grease a 9-by-13-inch baking pan with cooking spray and line pan with parchment (see page 221 for tips). Set aside.
2. In a saucepan over medium heat, melt butter, stirring occasionally, until milk solids turn deep golden brown. Remove from heat and transfer to a mixing bowl, scraping all the delicious browned bits from the pan. Let cool.
3. In a separate bowl, whisk together flour, baking powder, and salt.
4. Heat oven to 350°F. In the bowl of an electric mixer fitted with the paddle attachment, stir together cooled browned butter and both sugars. Add eggs and vanilla and beat on medium-high speed until light in color, about 3 minutes. Add flour mixture, walnuts, and toffee bits. Mix until thoroughly combined, then pour into prepared pan.
5. Bake until a cake tester inserted in the center comes out almost clean, 35 to 40 minutes. Do not overbake. Transfer to a wire rack to cool completely before removing from pan. Cut into squares to serve.

TARA'S TIP

It's less common than it used to be to find toffee bits in the baking section at the store. I order them online and store extra in the freezer. Toffee bits have nuts in them, so they can go rancid if stored improperly or for too long.

SERVES

16

MAKES

1 (9-BY-13-INCH)
PAN

HANDS-ON TIME

25 MINUTES

TOTAL TIME

1 HOUR 25 MINUTES

black-and-white butter bars

THINK ABOUT YOUR favorite song—the one you know all the lyrics to and can't help but dance to. If you could taste that joy and happiness . . . it would taste like these chocolatey butter bars. It's true!

With a hit of both white and semisweet chocolate chips (and by hit I mean a pound of each), these sweet and rich bar cookies can get anyone up and dancing. They are gloriously easy to make and get rave reviews. As noted by my taste-tester neighbors: "They were super good. Almost-brought-us-to-tears good."

---

1 cup (2 sticks) unsalted butter

1 pound white chocolate chips (about 2½ cups)

4 large eggs

1½ teaspoons plus a pinch fine salt, divided

1 cup granulated sugar

1 teaspoon vanilla extract

2 cups (256 g) all-purpose flour

1 pound semisweet chocolate chips (about 2½ cups)

---

1. Heat oven to 350°F and place the rack in the top third of the oven. Grease a 9-by-13-inch pan and line with parchment. Add clips to pan if desired (see page 221 for tips).

2. In a small saucepan on the stove or in a medium microwave–safe bowl in the microwave, melt butter. Remove from heat and add half (1¼ cups) the white chocolate chips. DO NOT STIR. Let sit 5 minutes, then whisk into a smooth mixture.

3. In a separate bowl with an electric mixer, beat eggs and a pinch salt. Add sugar and beat until pale yellow, about 3 minutes. Add white chocolate mixture, vanilla, and remaining 1½ teaspoons salt. Mix well.

4. Stir in flour and fold in remaining white chocolate chips and semisweet chocolate chips. Pour into prepared pan and bake until just set but still a little gooey, 35 to 40 minutes. Transfer pan to a wire rack to cool. Remove bars from pan and cut into squares to serve.

BAKING AND SWEETS

NOTE I've listed the cup measurement for the chocolate chips because they come in various sized packages, depending on the brand. You might need to buy several packages in order to measure the full pound (16 ounces) of each.

pb and fudge stripe freeze

INCREDIBLY SILKY, rich layers of peanut butter ice cream are layered on a peanut butter cookie crust with a layer of chocolate peanut butter fudge in the middle. This frozen dessert is a great make-ahead treat for a gathering, and you'll be surprised at how quiet the room gets once it's served. There may be a few "mmms" and "wows" as spoons clink on the plates, but other than that, this treat renders people quite speechless.

The hardest part of this recipe is waiting for the dessert to freeze!

COOKIE CRUMB LAYERS

28 Nutter Butter cookies, divided   ¼ cup butter, melted

CHOCOLATE PEANUT BUTTER FUDGE

1 cup milk chocolate chips   ¾ cup heavy cream

6 tablespoons smooth peanut butter   1 teaspoon vanilla extract

PEANUT BUTTER ICE CREAM

2½ quarts vanilla ice cream   1 cup smooth peanut butter

1. Line a 9-by-9-inch square baking pan with parchment with overhang and use clips to hold the parchment in place (see page 221 for tips).
2. For the cookie crumb layers: In a food processor, blend 20 Nutter Butter cookies until they are finely crushed. Add butter and pulse to combine. Reserve ¼ cup crumbs for the top of the dessert and press the rest into the bottom of the lined pan. Place pan in the freezer. Crumble remaining 8 cookies into small pieces and set aside.
3. For the fudge: In a medium saucepan over medium heat, whisk chocolate chips, peanut butter, and cream until chocolate is melted and cream is hot. Remove from heat and add vanilla extract. Transfer to a bowl to cool or place over an ice bath for a few minutes.
4. For the peanut butter ice cream: Scoop ice cream into an electric mixer fitted with the paddle attachment. Add peanut butter and blend until ice cream is smooth. Be careful—the ice cream likes to slide out of the bowl at first!
5. Working quickly, remove pan from freezer and spread half the peanut butter ice cream over the crust. Spread all but about ½ cup fudge over the ice cream. Sprinkle with broken Nutter Butter cookie pieces. Then spread remaining ice cream over the top. Drizzle with remaining fudge (I like to put it in a zip-top bag and snip the corner to pipe it on) and sprinkle with reserved ¼ cup crust crumbs. Immediately transfer pan to the freezer and freeze for at least 4 hours or overnight. After about 30 minutes you can remove the dessert, cover it with plastic wrap, and return it to the freezer for the rest of the 4 hours.
6. To serve, warm the edges of the pan with your hands, then use the parchment overhang to lift the dessert out of the pan and onto a cutting board. Slice into squares to serve.

SERVES

16

MAKES

1 (9-BY-9-INCH) PAN

HANDS-ON TIME

45 MINUTES

TOTAL TIME

4 HOURS
45 MINUTES

TARA'S TIP

Opt for creamy peanut butter right from the grocery store rather than a natural peanut butter. The classic store-bought version makes this dessert extra silky and delicious!

BAKING AND SWEETS

MAKES

8 LARGE COOKIES

HANDS-ON TIME

25 MINUTES

TOTAL TIME

50 MINUTES

great grains chocolate chip cookies

WHEN I WAS GROWING UP, the local bakery chain, known for their whole wheat bread, would sell giant whole-wheat-and-chocolate-chip cookies. Some of you may know the cookies of which I speak! When we picked up a loaf of bread, it was too tempting to not get a cookie to go. They were perfectly soft, not too cakey, and not too thin, with what might have been a hint of honey and just the right amount of chocolate chips (meaning loads!).

It's taken a lifetime to re-create a version worth sharing, and I think you'll agree. They are tempting and delicious, just like I remember.

1 cup (128 g) whole wheat flour	1 tablespoon honey
¼ teaspoon baking powder	1 teaspoon vanilla extract
¼ teaspoon baking soda	1 cup rolled oats
½ teaspoon fine salt	1 large egg
½ cup (1 stick) unsalted butter, softened	¾ cup milk chocolate chips
⅔ cup dark brown sugar	¾ cup semisweet chocolate chips

1. Heat oven to 325°F and line two baking sheets with parchment.
2. In a bowl, whisk together flour, baking powder, baking soda, and salt. Set aside.
3. In the bowl of an electric mixer fitted with the paddle attachment, combine butter, brown sugar, honey, and vanilla. Cream together on medium speed until just lightened, about 2 minutes.
4. Add oats and egg and blend until mixed well. Stir in flour mixture until just mixed in, and then add chocolate chips.
5. Divide dough into 8 portions (about ⅓ cup each) and place 4 on each baking sheet. Bake one sheet at a time until cookies are set and turning golden around the edges, 11 to 13 minutes. Let cookies cool on the pan. Cookies will keep airtight up to 3 days.

nyc snickerdoodles

NEW YORK CITY IS larger than life and has a bit of an attitude and some swagger. These giant, soft snickerdoodles follow suit. There's the buttery swagger with some tang from cream of tartar. I threw in some attitude and added a little bit of cinnamon to the batter (I know, blasphemous!), which enhances that essence in every bite. These cookies are super soft without being bland, and they have a genius sugary crisped edge. I think you'll agree we have a winner with these NYC-sized cookies!

MAKES

13 LARGE COOKIES

HANDS-ON TIME

30 MINUTES

TOTAL TIME

1 HOUR 15 MINUTES

2¼ cups (288 g) all-purpose flour

1¼ teaspoons cream of tartar

½ teaspoon baking soda

1½ teaspoons cinnamon, divided

½ teaspoon fine salt

1 cup (2 sticks) unsalted butter, room temperature

1¾ cups granulated sugar, divided

1 large egg, room temperature

2 teaspoons vanilla extract

1. In a bowl, whisk together flour, cream of tartar, baking soda, ½ teaspoon cinnamon, and salt. Set aside.

2. In the bowl of an electric mixer fitted with the paddle attachment, beat together butter and 1¼ cups sugar on medium speed until mixture is smooth and fluffy, about 1 minute. Add egg and vanilla and mix until completely combined. Add flour mixture and stir until combined well, scraping down the sides of the bowl as needed.

3. Scoop dough into ¼-cup-sized balls (or use a #16 cookie scoop) and place on a plate. Cover with plastic wrap and refrigerate 30 minutes or more.

4. Meanwhile, heat oven to 350°F and line baking sheets with parchment. In a small bowl, combine remaining ½ cup granulated sugar and remaining 1 teaspoon cinnamon.

5. After at least 30 minutes, roll chilled balls in your hand to smooth the shape, then roll in cinnamon sugar to coat. Place on baking sheets about 2 inches apart.

6. Bake until edges are golden and centers are puffed and just set, 11 to 13 minutes. To get the perfect wrinkled edge, bang the baking sheet on the countertop once or twice to settle the cookies. Slide the parchment with the cookies onto a cooling rack and let cool completely. Cookies can be stored airtight for up to 3 days.

NOTE To make 26 standard-sized cookies, scoop dough into 2-tablespoon balls using a #24-sized cookie scoop. Bake 9 to 10 minutes.

MAKES

12 LARGE COOKIES

HANDS-ON TIME

30 MINUTES

TOTAL TIME

1 HOUR 10 MINUTES

pecan double-chocolate-chunk cookies

I CONSIDER MYSELF a purist with chocolate chip cookies. I want just enough buttery dough to hold together the semisweet and milk chocolate morsels. Don't mess with perfection, right? But I'll make a few exceptions, and one is pecans. They add such a delicious, classic crunch to my favorite cookie.

This dough is rich with butter, brown sugar, and vanilla like you'd expect, and it includes my famous mix of dark and milk chocolate. They bake into chewy cookies with crispy edges, and the nutty bits of pecan add a welcome crunch.

Standard chocolate chips are great, but using chopped chocolate bars in their place is my preference here. Try it once and you'll see why. Biting into a cookie with large shards of oozy goodness is more of an experience than your standard cookie-jar snack.

TARA'S TIP

While chilling chocolate chip cookie dough is great and ideal with some recipes, this one is perfect baked immediately. The texture is still chewy and delicious.

1¾ cups (224 g) all-purpose flour	1 large egg, room temperature
¾ teaspoon baking powder	2 teaspoons vanilla extract
½ teaspoon baking soda	6 ounces (⅔ cup) large chunks semisweet chocolate, divided
1 teaspoon fine salt	
10 tablespoons unsalted butter, room temperature	6 ounces (⅔ cup) large chunks milk chocolate, divided
½ cup packed light brown sugar	¾ cup coarsely chopped pecans
½ cup granulated sugar	Flaky sea salt, if desired

1. Heat oven to 350°F. Line baking sheets with parchment. Set aside.

2. In a bowl, whisk together flour, baking powder, baking soda, and salt. Set aside.

3. In the bowl of an electric mixer fitted with the paddle attachment, beat butter and sugars together until smooth and well mixed, about 1 minute. Add egg and vanilla and mix well on medium speed, about 1 minute.

4. Stir in flour mixture, scraping down the sides of the bowl as needed. Set aside ¼ cup each of the chocolate chunks (for the cookie topping), then stir remaining chocolate chunks and pecans into dough.

5. Scoop dough into ¼-cup-sized balls (or use a #16 cookie scoop). Place on baking sheets about 2 inches apart. Nestle reserved pieces of chocolate on the top of each cookie. If you like salted cookies, sprinkle each ball with some sea salt flakes.

6. Bake until edges are golden and centers are just set, 12 to 14 minutes. Let cookies cool on baking sheets 1 or 2 minutes, then slide the parchment off the baking sheet and let cookies cool completely.

chocolate peanut butter puddle cookies

MAKES

10 LARGE COOKIES

HANDS-ON TIME

50 MINUTES

TOTAL TIME

1 HOUR 35 MINUTES

CUE THE MOON and the stars: Peanut butter and all the chocolate, please! These hand-sized rich chocolate cookies have a soft, brownie-like interior, little morsels of chocolate, and shards of homemade peanut butter chips that puddle right on top. The edges get just the right amount of crispiness, and the centers stay fudgy, so every bite is pretty heavenly.

You can use store-bought peanut butter chips, but I love taking an extra 10 minutes to make my own. Simply melt white chocolate, stir in peanut butter, spread on parchment to cool in the freezer, and chop. This method creates a chip (or chunk) with real peanut butter flavor, and the size makes those delightful pools of goodness on top of the cookie.

You can make them standard-cookie-sized or big bakery style (which is about ¼ cup of dough). Baking bigger cookies gives the gooey cookie lovers a few extra bites of heaven right in the center, and they are beautiful and fun to serve.

PEANUT BUTTER PUDDLE CHIPS

5 ounces white chocolate

6 tablespoons smooth peanut butter

COOKIES

1 cup (128 g) all-purpose flour

½ cup plus 2 tablespoons unsweetened cocoa powder (not Dutched)

1 teaspoon baking soda

½ teaspoon fine salt

½ cup (1 stick) unsalted butter, room temperature

⅓ cup granulated sugar

½ cup packed light brown sugar

1 large egg, room temperature

1 teaspoon vanilla extract

⅓ cup semisweet or milk chocolate chips or chunks

1. For the peanut butter puddle chips: Line a small baking sheet with parchment. In a microwave-safe bowl, melt white chocolate, stirring every 30 or 45 seconds. Stir in peanut butter until smooth and combined.

2. On prepared baking sheet, spread mixture into an 8-by-12-inch rectangle (about ⅜-inch thick). Freeze until solid, about 20 minutes, then score and chop into 1-inch pieces. Freeze pieces until you're ready to use them.

3. Heat oven to 350°F. Line two baking sheets with parchment. For the cookies: In a bowl, whisk together flour, cocoa powder, baking soda, and salt. Set aside.

4. In the bowl of an electric mixer fitted with the paddle attachment, beat butter and sugars until creamy, about 1 minute. Add egg and vanilla and beat until well mixed and lightened in color, another minute. Add flour mixture. Stir in chocolate chips, then remove bowl from the mixer.

Continued on next page

BAKING AND SWEETS

241

5. By hand, stir in all but 1 cup peanut butter puddle chips. Return the reserved peanut butter chips to the freezer.

6. Scoop dough into ¼-cup-sized balls (or use a #16 cookie scoop). Place about 2 inches apart on prepared baking sheets. Place reserved peanut butter chips on top of each ball, pressing them gently into the dough.

7. Bake cookies until edges are cooked and center has settled and is cooked through but not overdone, 10 to 12 minutes. If you would like, give the baking sheet a little bang or two on the countertop to flatten the cookies (optional). Let cookies cool on the baking sheet about 2 minutes, then slide the parchment off the baking sheet and let the cookies cool completely. Cookies will keep airtight up to 3 days.

Make peanut butter chips by melting white chocolate and peanut butter together. Spread on a parchment-lined baking sheet. Chill in the freezer.

Score and chop chilled peanut butter mixture into 1-inch squares. Return chips to the freezer until ready to use.

SERVES

8 TO 10

MAKES

1 (9-INCH) TART

HANDS-ON TIME

30 MINUTES

TOTAL TIME

3 HOURS

passion fruit meringue tart with coconut cookie crust

THIS DESSERT TASTES like the tropics! You'll love the passion-fruit flavor, and the meringue topping is luxurious and smooth. Serve this tart at spring parties, for summer gatherings, or as one of your Thanksgiving pies.

If you don't have a tart pan, press the crust into a standard 8- or 9-inch pie pan. Just adjust the cooking time to make sure the filling is set.

CRUST

18 graham cracker sheets

¼ cup confectioners' sugar

¾ cup sweetened shredded coconut, (toasted)

9 tablespoons butter, melted

FILLING AND TOPPING

4 eggs, separated, whites covered and stored in the refrigerator

1¼ cups granulated sugar, divided

1 (14-ounce) can sweetened condensed milk

½ cup pure passion fruit purée or concentrate

2 tablespoons fresh lime juice

Pinch salt

1. For the crust: Heat oven to 325°F. In a food processor, blend crackers, confectioners' sugar, and coconut until finely ground. Add butter and blend. In a 9-inch tart pan with removable bottom, press mixture firmly into bottom and all the way up the sides. Place pan on a baking sheet for stability and bake until lightly browned, 12 to 15 minutes. Let cool. Unfilled crust can be stored loosely covered with foil up to 1 day.

2. For the filling: With an electric mixer, beat egg yolks and ¼ cup sugar until thick and light in color, about 4 minutes. Stir in sweetened condensed milk and mix another 2 minutes. Stir in passion fruit purée and lime juice. Pour mixture into crust and bake until just set in the center when gently shaken, 20 to 25 minutes. Cool tart completely, then refrigerate at least 1 hour or up to 4 hours before topping and serving.

3. For the meringue topping: In a mixing bowl set over a pan of simmering water, whisk together egg whites, remaining 1 cup sugar, and salt. When sugar is dissolved and mixture is hot to the touch, remove from heat. With an electric mixer, whip until firm peaks form, about 12 minutes. Transfer to a piping bag fitted with a #826 large open star tip. Pipe some meringue onto chilled pie. Alternatively, just spoon some meringue on the tart in dollops. Set under a broiler until just toasted or use a brûlée torch to toast the top of the meringue. Top with extra toasted coconut to garnish if desired (see Tara's Tip on page 191).

NOTE You'll have extra meringue. You can discard it or pipe dollops onto a parchment-lined baking sheet to make crispy meringue kisses. Bake at 225°F for 90 minutes. Turn off oven and let cool in oven 1 hour.

maple hazelnut pie

DECADENT NUT PIES like a gooey pecan pie are special holiday desserts, and this one certainly fits in that category. I use hazelnuts and add luscious maple syrup plus an extra sprinkle of salt into the caramel filling to give it that salted-caramel flavor we all love.

The hazelnuts are special and indulgent, and a dollop of sweetened whipped cream brings everything together on this truly gorgeous pie.

SERVES

8 TO 10

MAKES

1 (9-INCH) PIE

HANDS-ON TIME

30 MINUTES

TOTAL TIME

4 HOURS
30 MINUTES

PIE CRUST

1 crust from Classic Pie Crust (page 227), prepared but not baked (see step 1 below)

MAPLE HAZELNUT FILLING

1 cup pure maple syrup

⅔ cup packed light brown sugar

⅔ cup light corn syrup

¾ teaspoon fine salt

6 tablespoons unsalted butter, cut into pieces

1½ teaspoons vanilla extract

4 large eggs

2½ cups husked hazelnuts, divided

CREAM TOPPING

1 cup heavy cream

3 tablespoons confectioners' sugar

½ teaspoon vanilla extract

> **TARA'S TIP**
>
> A traditional pie crimp is beautiful, but if you're feeling fancy, I used the second crust from my pie dough recipe to make a braid for my pie edge. Roll it out, cut many thin strips, and gently braid them together. Use egg wash to adhere the braid to your edge.

1. For the crust: On a lightly floured surface, roll dough to a 12-inch circle and gently transfer to a 9-inch pie pan. Decorate edge as desired and place in freezer until ready to fill.

2. For the filling: Heat oven to 350°F with rack in the lower third.

3. In a medium saucepan over medium heat, bring maple syrup, brown sugar, corn syrup, and salt to a boil, stirring until sugar dissolves. Then boil 1 minute more, reducing heat as needed to prevent mixture from boiling over.

4. Remove pan from heat. Add butter and vanilla and stir until butter melts. Let cool to lukewarm. Chop 2 cups husked hazelnuts and set aside.

5. In a mixing bowl, beat eggs until frothy. Whisk in cooled maple syrup mixture.

6. Spread chopped hazelnuts in prepared crust and cover with filling. Add remaining ½ cup whole hazelnuts on top.

7. Bake pie until filling is set and slightly puffed, about 1 hour, covering crust with foil for the last 20 minutes to prevent overbrowning. Cool completely before serving, about 3 hours. Baked pie can be covered and stored at room temperature for up to a day.

8. For cream topping: When ready to serve, whip cream with confectioners' sugar until soft peaks form. Add vanilla. Serve with pie.

NOTE If you can't find husked (also called skinned or blanched) hazelnuts, you can remove the brown skins yourself. The husk is fine to eat, but I remove as much as I can just for looks in this recipe. Toast hazelnuts in a 350°F oven about 7 minutes, then immediately place in a clean kitchen towel and rub vigorously. Quite a bit of the husk should peel off this way.

ACKNOWLEDGMENTS

Delicious Gatherings is in your hands because of many people and many hours of working, cooking, editing, and designing. I'm so grateful for everyone who made this cookbook possible because it means I am able to share some of my favorite tastes, memories, and food with you in a most beautiful and tangible form!

This book is thanks to my mom, Mary, who taught me to cook, inspired my first book, *Live Life Deliciously*, and made this one possible with countless hours of recipe testing, dish washing, grocery shopping, and manuscript reading. She also assisted on photo shoots, typed up notes, and offered words of motivation. Thank you to my dad for visits, babysitting, listening, and supporting me throughout the process. And to my siblings, extended family, neighbors, and dear friends for tasting my creations and giving me hugs—both real and virtual—and pats on the back.

Thanks to my favorite creative partners, Ty Mecham and Veronica Olson, for bringing my ideas to fruition and making them look better than I ever could have imagined. To my food team, Ayelet Davids, Mary and Marie Bench, Nancy Kochan, Lindsey Hargett, and Laura Arnold, who know what to do and what is best before I do. Thank you for making me laugh and enjoy that part of the process. And thank you to all the recipe testers who spent their time helping make these recipes the best they could be.

A heartfelt thank-you to my Tara Teaspoon team: Amy, Britney, Megan, Lindsay, Misty, and Julie, who have kept things going while I worked endlessly on the book. Thanks to Carrie, Troy, and Callie for getting this book out in the world in an exciting way.

Thank you to my heroes in publishing, Chris, Heather, Heidi, Lisa, Richard, and Ashlin, for championing another cookbook, for their patience in the time-consuming, back-and-forth of editing and designing, and for their attention to the details that are important to me so that something beautiful and enriching could be shared.

Thanks to Grapes from California for sponsoring and supporting this book and for being an advocate and partner in this delightful food space.

A loving thanks to the TaraTeaspoon.com readers, social followers, commenters, and emailers who inspire my work every day and who are the behind-the-scenes support of my business.

PHOTO INDEX

SERIOUS SIDES

BBQ Baked Beans

Golden Sweet Cornbread

Grape and Feta Quinoa

Roast Carrots with Lemon Feta Dip

Spinach and Artichoke Tarte Soleil

Asparagus and Peas with Parmesan Breadcrumbs

Loaded Guacamole Dip

Pepper Jack Nacho Cheese

Chili Cheese Fries

The Ultimate Chili con Queso

Avocado Salad

Easy French Bread

Buttery Rice Pilaf with Vermicelli

Cauliflower and Couscous Gratin

Crispy and Spicy Harissa Potatoes with Yogurt

Creamy Garlic-and-Herb Mac and Cheese

MAIN EVENTS

123
Skirt Steak with Strawberry Chimichurri and Rice Pilaf

124
Italian Gnocchi, Bacon, and Cheese Soup

127
Chicken Banh Mi Burgers

128
Red Beans and Rice with Avocado Salad

131
Quick Marinara

133
Pasta with Brussels Sprouts and Walnut-Sage Browned Butter

134
Sweet-and-Savory Grilled Chicken Sandwich

137
Blue-Ribbon Beef-and-Bacon Chili

138
"Creamy" Tomato and White Bean Soup

141
Giant Dinner Meatballs

142
Three-Cheese and Zucchini Ravioli Pillows

145
Spicy Chorizo and Tomato Pasta

146
Mamma Mia! Red Pepper and Burrata Burgers

149
White Pesto Pasta with Spicy Broccoli

150
Wild Mushroom and Spinach Risotto

153
Thai Coconut Chicken and Rice Noodle Soup

155
Texas-Style Beef Brisket at Home

158
Blackened Salmon with Mango-Lime Salsa

161
Salmon and Arugula Pasta

162
Spicy Honey-Lime Chicken

164
Salsa Verde Chicken Enchiladas

167
Greek Chicken Meatballs with Lemon Orzo and Tzatziki

New York
Chocolate Babka
173

Half-and-Half Granola
Pancakes with Ginger
Maple Cream Syrup
177

Diner Breakfast
Potatoes
179

Brûléed Oatmeal
180

Family Breakfast
Turnover
183

Churro Waffles with
Whipped Ricotta and
Dulce de Leche
184

Easy Hash Brown
Breakfast Bake
187

Cinnamon-Sugar,
Almond, and
Ricotta Bread Pudding
188

Coconut Cream
Sweet Rolls
191

Perfect Lemon
Loaf Cake
194

Blueberry Bannock
Scone
197

Cheesecake-Topped
Whole-Wheat
Brown Sugar Muffins
200

Blackberry and Lemon
Curd Swirled Ice Cream

Coconut Bundt Cake

Blackberry and Peach
Cornbread Shortcake

Apple Pudding Cake
with Butter Sauce

Secret Chocolate Cake

Chilled Strawberries-
and-Cream Soufflé

Sunken Chocolate
Cakes with
Hot Fudge Sauce

Fresh Peach Pie with
Sweet Cream Cheese

Classic Pie Crust

Browned-Butter
Toffee Blondies

Black-and-White
Butter Bars

PB and Fudge
Stripe Freeze

Great Grains Chocolate
Chip Cookies

NYC Snickerdoodles

Pecan Double-
Chocolate-Chunk
Cookies

Chocolate Peanut
Butter Puddle Cookies

Passion Fruit Meringue
Tart with Coconut
Cookie Crust

Maple Hazelnut Pie

INDEX